Joris Ivens
50 years of film-making

Rosalind Delmar

1979

Educational Advisory Service
British Film Institute
127 Charing Cross Road, London WC2H OEA

Joris Ivens has produced some of the most important contributions to
political cinema during the last 50 years, with films like *Song of the Rivers,
Spanish Earth, A Valparaiso* and *How Yukong Moved the Mountains*. This
introductory study includes articles on his work, an extensive biofilmography, and extracts from the film-texts.

The author
Rosalind Delmar teaches at the North London Polytechnic and is a
freelance writer. She is particularly interested in the relationship between
politics and cinema and, among her writings, she has contributed an article
on Chinese cinema to *Screen*.

ISBN 0 85170 092 6

Contents

Acknowledgements

I should like to thank Mark Nash for suggesting that I work on Ivens; Jan de Vaal and the staff of the Amsterdam Filmmuseum for making it possible for me to see films not available in London; Joris Ivens for taking time off from a crowded schedule to talk about his work; Bert Hogenkamp for putting his own work at my disposal; the staff of the BFI Information library, in particular Gillian Hartnoll and Susan Huxley; Terry Dennett for producing frame stills from *Misére au Borinage;* Jeanne Hadfield for producing transcripts of *Spanish Earth* and *Song of the Rivers;* Liz Heron, E.G. Noujain and Michael Chanan for translations; Geoffrey Nowell-Smith for help with the bibliography; Angela Martin for her editorial work; Ian Christie and Colin McArthur for useful information. None of these people are at all responsible for the final contents of this booklet, or for its faults.

We should also like to acknowledge L'Avant-Scène Cinéma; the BFI Stills Library; Capi-Films; Cinéma Politique; Cinéma 64 and 70; Dennis Dobson (publishers of Bela Balazs, *Theory of the Film*); Les Editeurs Français Réunis; Filméditions (publishers of A Zalzman, *Joris Ivens*); Filmfaust; Film Quarterly; Stanley Foreman; J Prévert, *Choses et autres* Copyright © Editions Gallimard 1972; Stan Hugill; Image et Son; Joris Ivens; Jeune Cinéma; Les Lettres Françaises; Positif; La Revue des Vivants; Seven Seas Books (publishers of *The Camera and I*); der Staatlichen Film Archiv der DDR and Helen van Dongen for material used in the book.

Introduction

Joris Ivens has been working with film for fifty years now, but his work is little known in Britain and few of his films are as yet available here. His film series *How Yukong Moved the Mountains* (1975) is perhaps the best known, parts being shown on BBC TV in 1977. So that where an idea of Ivens' work exists, it is often related to his most recent films. He works, too, in the area of documentary cinema, which has never been 'box-office'; and throughout his working life he has been politically committed to the left, and more censored for this than most. It would be impossible to give a full account of his fifty years of film-making in a single introduction. Instead I shall aim to discuss some characteristics of his approach, in the hope that a contribution might be made to current re-appraisal and discussion of the documentary form.

Objectivity
Mainly as a result of the extensive use made by television of documentary and the existence of rules within the BBC, for example, to define the permissible within documentary, preliminary discussion of this form often revolves around questions of 'objectivity'. The demand for objectivity is often, if crudely, put as a demand that 'both sides of the argument' should be represented. This is not a new demand, but has become much more widely diffused through broadcasting practice. There are several aspects to this demand. The posing of issues as having 'two sides' and rarely more implies strict division and the existence of the dominant and the opposi-tional view: the film-maker is requested to be outside of this division, but capable of incorporating both. The demand is usually made about areas of politics and history – for example, it is rarely made about cultural products: the demand to hear both sides of the argument on Mahler, Picasso or Christopher Wren would be an extremely unusual one. This is because settling these issues is not seen to be of major public concern, and because in the realm of culture a consensus is often safely assumed to exist. Where consensus is being broken, or disrupted, however, this demand comes into its own. Indeed, it is usually to the *breakers* of the consensus that the demand is addressed. But in either case one point of view is asked to prove its 'objectivity' by demonstrating its capacity to incorporate the opposition.

Any preliminary study of Ivens' political and historical films reveals that Ivens himself subscribes to the idea that there is a structure of opposition, of

1

conflict, of sides, but that rather than believing that both should be represented within his films, his practice is to take sides (*Spanish Earth, Borinage, 400 Million* are examples). The documentary film-maker who responds to the call of objectivity almost certainly prepares himself to fall into the position of a judge (if not, the result is confusion) and, as judge, can pass on that position to the spectator. Ivens' approach is perhaps more modest than this. He does not set out to weigh all arguments in the balance and deliver judgment, but to act as a witness. Yet a witness has his own objectivity. He gives evidence of what he saw and the conclusions he reached, and gives this evidence to the best of his ability. The witness is an actor in a court-room drama which has two sides: prosecution and defence. Ivens, through his films, has often appeared as witness for the prosecution: the prosecution of America in Vietnam, of Japan in China, and so on. But he has been a witness in a political-historical drama in which the prosecution of one side is also the defence of another. His films have aspired not to represent 'the whole truth', but a part of the truth, with all the means at his disposal. The most important means at his disposal was the camera.

The Camera-Eye
The 'objectivity' of the witness takes subjectivity into account. The 'I saw', 'I heard' this or that is immediately produced. Ivens grew up amongst cameras, apparatuses which have a privileged place in relation to the 'seeing I'. His first film, made at eleven, was possible because he came from a family of photographic experts, and his early life, education and film experience was dedicated to acquiring knowledge about how the camera worked.

The camera can act sometimes as a surrogate eye, sometimes as a third eye. Amongst Ivens' early experiments there was the attempt to develop a subjective use of the camera, to make the camera take the place of the eye of its manipulator. These attempts failed, but left their mark. In *Zuiderzee*, during the sequence of closure of the main dyke (a sequence repeated in *New Earth*), different camera set-ups identify with the different protagonists – land, sea and machine directed by man. In *Borinage* the camera attempts to join in the demonstration at Wasmes, where the portrait of Karl Marx is carried through the streets. In the earlier *Breakers* (1929), the camera had at one point tried to take the place of the sea as it washed its shores; in these later films the camera participates in the action, as a form of identification. After *Spanish Earth* Ivens stopped acting as camera operator and became director, but the camera was always expected to be active. The moment of separation from the camera had perhaps taken place, but the camera-eye was still a presence. This is valid even when editing takes over, and shapes and places what the camera has recorded.

The term 'camera-eye' is redolent of the twenties and thirties. As a conception it derives from Dziga Vertov, whose notion of film-making was extremely different from that of Ivens. It has associations, too, with

2

Isherwood's *'I am a Camera'*, and re-appears, in different form, in the title of Ivens' autobiography, *The Camera and I*. As aspiration it takes its place within a segment of the documentary movement of the thirties: that part of the movement which sought to bear 'eye-witness'.

Social documentary is only one genre amongst others which appeared in the 1930s. What was held in common was their testimony to first-hand experience. Steinbeck's *Grapes of Wrath* was valued because 'he had really been there'. Another new form was the documentary book which set first-hand descriptions alongside photographic records, whose purpose was to prove the validity of the written word, itself suspected of instability and unreliability. Social consciousness was combined with the visual in an extremely direct way. And if the products of that period can be easily criticised for a too easy acceptance of an equation between seeing and believing, that only indicates their acknowledgment of the immense power of the visual in forming consciousness. Much of Ivens' production, from *Borinage* to *Le ciel, la terre*, has taken the form of an 'eye-witness' account. It should not be concluded, however, that within his work there is a reliance on the empiricism of the reportage. For the equation seeing and believing produces an anxiety – an anxiety about the authenticity of what is seen. Ivens' work, however, has been concerned with making visible what is not seen.

Authenticity
The desire for authenticity is a desire for reassurance that everything shown in a film happened spontaneously whilst the camera was there. As absolute demand, it can rarely be achieved. In Ivens' case, although in his war films, like *Spanish Earth*, there is a guarantee of authenticity, in others he has been prepared to use re-enactments.

The purpose of such re-enactments is to convey emotional meaning or to show important points about a situation which might not otherwise be immediately available at the time of filming. The biofilmography contains material on re-enactment – in *Borinage, Komsomol, New Earth* and others.

The main point here is to make clear that Ivens has never contributed to the cult of authenticity. Authenticity is one element in his work, but not its totality. It is a component in films which are highly constructed, and often mingle different forms of material. *Borinage* contains newsreel footage (the Ambridge sequence) and re-enactment (the demonstration at Wasmes). They co-exist with other material in a film which welds all its elements together into a single statement: a statement about a process (exploitation and the antagonism between capital and labour) which is only observable through its effects. In this sense, the events recorded have symptomatic value. They cannot be read off as 'reality' itself, but as pointers to a reality which is not easily accessible. *Borinage*, too, is a film which was made in conditions of semi-clandestinity and intense political repression. All forms of organisation did not – and would not – necessarily occur at the time the

3

film-makers were there. But their absence at one moment did not negate their presence at another. The film aims to portray as many aspects as possible of the situation addressed; the recourse to re-enactment, therefore, is explicable.

On the other hand, 'authenticity' has many different possible meanings. Ivens does have an attachment to a conception of emotional and political authenticity, greater perhaps than any attachment to naturalism or empiricism. The documentary movement, moreover, embraces diverse types of film practice, just as Ivens has produced many different kinds of films. Neither the genre, nor this particular film-maker, can be summed up by a single formula. At the beginning of the documentary stands the figure of Flaherty, about one of whose films, *Moana,* the term 'documentary' was first used, by Grierson in 1924.

Flaherty is a problematic figure because although he had a conception of spiritual authenticity, he by no means subscribed to 'authenticity' in its popular meaning. If he wanted his men of Aran to fish in a particular way, he taught them how; if he wanted a father and son for *Louisiana Story,* he chose two local people and made them into father and son for the purposes of his film. For these sorts of reasons some people would claim that Flaherty cannot be counted among the documentarists, even if he still remains a great film-maker. This still leaves out of account, however, the amount of borrowing and learning which goes on between different film forms. Too much discussion of re-enacted scenes can deflect attention from the role of editing and sound, elements which also create meaning, and which, moreover, take over when the filming is over.

Narrative, editing, sound

Ivens studied editing, according to his account in *The Camera and I,* by borrowing films shown by the Dutch Film League, and making shot-by-shot breakdowns in order to analyse the rhythm. He was helped, of course, by his position as technical director of his father's firm and the availability of equipment. When he began to make his own films he invented his own method of editing. His skill as an editor is one of the reasons why he was appreciated by the Russian film-makers who invited him to the Soviet Union. It is interesting that the films he cites as examples came from the Soviet Union, and were also fictional – one a reconstruction. They are Dovzhenko's *Arsenal* and Eisenstein's *Potemkin.*

What emerges in Ivens' first experimental films – *Rain* and *The Bridge* – is not just the skill at editing, and the research into the vocabulary of movement, but also a strong narrative drive. Ivens constructs these films like a story, and gives narrative unity – not *a priori* to be expected from experimentalism. Unity is created by the construction of narrative time.

It is possible to look at *Rain* and then write, as Pierre Michaut did in *Cahiers du Cinéma,* about 'the afternoon of *Rain*'. The material for *Rain* was, of course, collected over time, from many different showers. In its final

4

form the film is structured to give the impression of a single rain-shower, with a beginning – the warning signs; a middle – the shower and its effects; and a happy ending – the rain stops, the sun comes out. The rain has introduced an element of disorder (like the wind in *Pour le Mistral*); at the end order is restored.

In *The Bridge*, again shot over a long period, a narration is also produced. A train approaches the bridge, but is arrested in its motion by the movement of the bridge which allows a ship to pass underneath. When the bridge returns to its original position the obstacle is removed. The driver blows the whistle and the train is off again. Its movement is completed.

This structure of movement/obstacle or disruption/triumphant completion of the action, is common ground between Ivens' construction of many of his films and 'the fiction film'. The form plays itself out, however, in a different way; the psychodrama between experiencing subjects is displaced on to the drama of the relationship between different elements. There is an imaginary subject in *The Bridge* – the train – but the train is not a person. All the same the problem of the train's activity adds energy in the playing out of the story as far as the spectator is concerned.

A later example of a construction of narrative time which creates or conveys meaning can be found in *Power and the Land*. In this film, whose object is to show the benefits of an American rural electrification programme, the day without electricity is much longer – takes more film time – than the day with it. In this way a particular meaning of the 'shorter working day' is conveyed: a day which contains lighter, easier work. It is a conception and use of film which is far removed from any ambition to record 'actual' events. The preoccupation is with giving them a structure.

Ivens has always taken great care in his editing, both from the point of view of structure and order and from the point of view of its function as director of the spectator's gaze. In 'Subjektivität und Montage' he commented: 'The two most important things to note about *New Earth* are: 1. that every shot has a critical duration; 2. the attempt to work from where the chief interest of the gaze of the spectator lies. If it is directed towards the left corner, I build my next shot up from the left. If I wanted to disturb the spectator, I then might do the opposite. If I wanted to make the spectator aware of the conflict between land and sea, I built my shots up from opposing sides of the screen. I have always attempted to have a basis on which to direct the gaze of the spectator.'

Not just image, but sound too is the object of careful construction, of analytic editing. The sound-tracks of his first sound films are compositions. Sounds needed are broken down and then reconstructed in the sound studio. Several sounds were combined to make one scream in *The Spanish Earth*. Helen van Dongen described her sound-track work as being like 'electronic music . . . a combination of things that you have to invent and make, reassemble, and finally you get the effect you want.' There is no question of naturalism here. Nor even when the use of camera-synched

5

sound is possible.

A notable feature of *How Yukong Moved the Mountains* is the careful enunciation of different voices and different forms of speech on the sound-track. Every element can be distinctly heard – the French question, its translation into Chinese, the answer in Chinese, the French translation, and the English translation, are all separately present.

Because of his early formation in silent cinema and his work in a variety of conditions where only a silent camera was available (as late as 1965, in Vietnam, he was working with a silent camera) Ivens might be expected to neglect the aspect of sound. In fact this is not so. There are many features of his approach to sound, in particular to the commentary. He often uses professional writers, craftsmen like himself in their own field, from Ernest Hemingway to Jacques Prévert. He often tries to capture local speech: Peter Finch speaks as an Australian in *Indonesia Calling; L'Italia non é un paese povero* contains passages in local dialect, unusual even now in the Italian cinema. The place and the positioning of the narrator is also of interest.

When *Spanish Earth* was made it was intended to rally support. Big names were looked for to record the commentary, and one approach was made to Orson Welles, who agreed. Welles was at the height of his radio career, and epitomised the voice of authority and truth. His broadcast *War of the Worlds* created a panic, and people rushed into the street, believing the announcement of an invasion from Mars. But his style did not suit *The Spanish Earth* and Hemingway re-recorded his own commentary. The voice of authority had to be discarded, and in its place was put a voice which spoke to the audience in many different ways, as interpreter, guide, spokesman, and next-door neighbour. Ivens' commentators speak with many voices. They denounce, reflect, proclaim, urge, argue to and with the spectator. But they seldom put a simple truth. His most obviously didactic film, *Le peuple et ses fusils,* is most didactic in its silent inter-titles. The function of the commentary more often than not is to put a point of view. The point of view relates to the exposition of certain themes, which run through Ivens' work.

Themes

A constant object of Ivens' attention is man at work. This fascination with work takes two main forms: first, the struggle to transform nature; second, the mechanics of the labour process. The theme of the struggle to control nature is a complex one. First, there is the aspect of the struggle for *political* control over territory: this ranges from *The Spanish Earth* and internal conflict – 'For fifty years we've wanted to irrigate, but they held us back' – to *How Yukong Moved the Mountains,* where a successful national struggle for liberation precedes a new struggle to tame the elements and channel resources. Then there is the theme of reclamation, of man winning territory from nature. The most striking example of this is *Zuiderzee,* with its dramatic battle between men and their machines, the land, and the sea – the land in this case being an ally of man against the sea. Nature as product and object of human labour is also a central theme of *Song of the Rivers*. There is also the aspect of a movement from subsistence to surplus. The potential of the magnetic mountain near Magnitogorsk is depicted in a futuristic animation sequence of an abundance of tractors in *Komsomol*; the Chinese symbol of abundance, the fish, is given attention in the final sequence of *Before Spring*; the drama of the Bulgarian episode of *The First Years* is linked to final liberation from dependence on nature – dependence, that is, on its arbitrary power to create drought.

The mechanics of the labour process are depicted in many of Ivens' films, but perhaps most strikingly in *Philips-Radio*. There the fragmentation of assembly-line production is explored most consistently. Where, in other films, the useful effects of co-operation are depicted, here the negative effects of a breaking down of productive elements into their component parts is placed in the foreground.

With a film-maker as interested in work as Ivens, it is worth looking more closely at the type of work depicted. In agriculture, it is usually pacific – pastoral or arable, the production of rice, wheat, milk – rarely meat or fish. This choice of material takes on added significance when those engaged in the work are faced with external aggression: it allows the aggressor to be more easily identified with violence. In industry the most resonant themes are those of the extraction of raw material like coal, oil, and their immediate transformation into steel, plastics, fuel. The use of natural resources tends to be paramount. Their waste is depicted as a crime.

The aspect of social relations (class, exploitation, etc.) is thus closely tied, in Ivens' work, to a basic symbolic of nature, seen both in itself and as a resource for man. Nature appears symbolised through the elements – earth, air, fire and water – which are further linked to the world of man by often being sexualised.

I have attempted, in this introduction, to point to those elements of Ivens' work which stress the richness and complexity of construction he has developed over a long and varied career. The specific relationship of his formal concerns to the subject matter of his films is discussed in the biofilmography which follows, with considerable quoted material from Ivens himself and the people who worked with him.

R.D.

Joris Ivens: Biofilmography

The best writer about Joris Ivens' work has been Joris Ivens himself. No other piece of work could take the place of *The Camera and I*, for example, and it is not the intention of this biofilmography to attempt it. Instead, it starts on the basis of a hypothesis, which is that to be able to make films almost continuously over fifty years, as Joris Ivens has done, is a remarkable achievement which can only have been made possible by the existence of an environment which encouraged and supported Ivens in his projects and by the film-maker's capacity to seize opportunities presented. For this reason, this biofilmography aims to give an indication of the ground on which Ivens' films have been appreciated over such a long period (the reasons, of course, are often different); the political reality into which his films were inserted and from which inspiration was often drawn; and to provide glimpses of the production conditions within which the work took place.

Roland Barthes has pointed out that once one treats of the author, one inevitably treats of the critic. In the case of Ivens, although continuity is given by his directing force in most of his films, many of his collaborators have affirmed how closely they were allowed – and expected – to participate in the filmatic construction. For this reason the points of view of various collaborators – Helen van Dongen, Hanns Eisler, Georges Sadoul, among others – are included, as 'co-authors' whose comments can contribute to the assessment of various of Ivens' films. Where reviews from film-critics are included,

8

they are intended, again, to amplify the value attached to his work. This seemed particularly important since the body of his work is so little known in England.

Finally it should be pointed out that this biofilmography is in itself an interpretation. It is not offered as an authoritative statement but as a tool, a point of entry. There are may ways of approaching Ivens' cinema, and this is simply one of them.

1 Childhood and education

Joris Ivens was born on November 18, 1898, into a family which had been involved with photographic processes for two generations. His grandfather had introduced the daguerreotype into Holland, and his father was head of the family photographic business, CAPI (Cornelius, Adrian, Peter Ivens). It was partly as a result of Joris Ivens' involvement with film that the firm later expanded into film production, being co-producer of many of his films including his most recent film series *How Yukong Moved the Mountains*.

Ivens made his first film at the age of 13, using members of his family as the cast, and shooting it around the family home in Nijmegen.

1911: **Brandende Straal** or **De Wigwam** (Wigwam) Holland
Cast
Joris Ivens: Brandende Straal (*Shining Ray*); Willem Ivens: Zwarte Adelaar (*Black Eagle*); Peter Ivens: The Father; Dorothea Ivens: The Mother; Hans Ivens: a child; Theodora Ivens: a child; Jacoba Ivens: the kidnapped child.
7 mins. b/w 35mm.

'At eleven my favourite books were about Indians, books by James Fenimore Cooper and Karl May. The latter, a German writer who had never been in America, wrote about "good" Indians exclusively. That was what we preferred.

'There was a "white elephant" in my father's shop – a professional Pathé cinema camera, wooden and hand-cranked, that my father despaired of selling to the citizens of Nijmegen. It was not a difficult transition from playing our Indian games outside the town to thinking up an Indian film for our own fun. The old Pathé camera was the spur. I organised my two brothers and my sister and my parents, and naturally myself, as a double cast of Indians and whites. When playing Indian roles our make-up was good Dutch chocolate powder. As the Indian hero, my head ornament was made of stolen turkey feathers. The landscape exteriors turned out splendidly with sandhills and heather fields doing duty as the Mojave desert and the Rocky Mountains. Even an old white horse played a romantic role in the sandhills. But we forgot to take his close-up. This we had to do weeks later in the garden of our house where I brought the big white horse straight through the narrow marble corridor of our good "burgher" home, his old

9

flanks scraping the walls on both sides of all pictures and gaslight fixtures –
meeting my first film production problem. My mother always had less
pleasure than the rest of us at our screenings . . .' ('Apprentice to Films'
Joris Ivens, *Theatre Arts*, March 1946)

Ivens' education was designed with his future participation in the family
business in mind, and in 1917 he was sent to the Rotterdam College of
Economics. After a semester he was mobilised for war service, but saw no
fighting, as Holland remained neutral during the 1914–18 War. With the
end of the War he finished his economics course, and then was sent to
Germany, to the University of Charlottenburg, to study photo-chemistry.

   Post-war Germany, and in particular post-war Berlin, was the scene of
intense political activity and also of intense cultural development, from
expressionism to Dada, the theatre of Piscator, the music of Schoenberg
and Eisler. It was also a time of inflation, and Ivens was able to use his
Dutch money to become a spectator of these new developments in German
culture. Hanns Eisler was a musician with whom he later collaborated on
several films, and Bertolt Brecht another product of this Berlin culture with
whom he also later worked.

   When inflation diminished, and finances became tight, Ivens moved to
Dresden and then to Jena, working in camera factories – Ica and Ernemann
in Dresden, Zeiss in Jena. His first experimental films, *Bridge* and *Rain*
were shot using an Ica Kinamo, a cheap camera (costing about £18 in 1928)
with limited resources – it would take only one hundred feet of film at a
time, and mixes and fades in the camera were impossible – but sufficient for
his purposes. Whilst in Dresden and Jena he saw films by Pabst and
Murnau, although, as he wrote later: 'I never identified these complex
productions of studio and theatre with my own life.' (Joris Ivens, *The
Camera and I*, p. 18)

   In 1926, after four years in Germany, he returned to Amsterdam,
becoming manager of the Amsterdam branch of CAPI and head of the firm's
technical department.

2 The years of the Film League: 1927–32

Ivens' interest in and involvement with avant-garde artistic and film circles
continued. The model of independent cinema production and distribution
in the mid-twenties (as often now) lay in production by small groups of
individuals, rather than studio production, and distribution through
cinemas or societies devoted to such films. The *Studio des Ursulines* in Paris
was the model for the rest of Europe – for Film Societies in London and
Berlin as much as for the Dutch Film League of which Ivens was a founder
member. The film critic Bryher, writing in *Close Up*, one of the most
influential film magazines of the avant-garde of that period, based her

principles of film club organisation on the experience of the *Ursulines*. These were: 'No censorship. Films to be shown in the original version as cut by their directors. Two-thirds of the films shown each season should be new, for six months in the cinema may mean revolution of lighting or photographic method.' (Bryher, 'How I would start a Film Club', *Close Up*, Vol. II, No. 6, June 1928)

The issue of censorship was felt to be extremely important, and the impetus for the Dutch Film League (Filmliga) came from the banning of Pudovkin's *Mother* from public distribution in Holland. Ivens borrowed a projector from his father's shop and showed the film four times during one evening in the Amsterdam artists' club De Kring. The Filmliga was formed shortly afterwards to make similar showings possible. Their manifesto, with its emphasis on cinema as art, and the opposition posited between art and commerce, is typical of the resistance to Hollywood at that time.

Extract from Filmliga Manifesto

FILM IS AT STAKE

Once in a hundred times we see film, the rest of the time we see movies.
The herd, commercial clichés, America, Kitsch.
In this arena films and movies are natural opponents. We believe in the pure autonomous film. The future of film as art is doomed if we do not take the matter into our own hands.
This is what we intend to do.

We want to see the experimental work produced in the French, German and Russian avant-garde ateliers.
We want to work towards film criticism that is in itself original, constructive and independent.
We have therefore founded

FILMLIGA AMSTERDAM

for the purpose of showing to limited audiences those films one does not see in the movie theatres or which one discovers by accident.
We have one advantage: good films are not expensive, for the very reason that they are not in demand. Good films lie profitless in the vaults of Paris and Berlin. We will buy these.' (September 1927, Joris Ivens, *The Camera and I*, p.21)

The Filmliga was an enormous success, branches being set up in other cities and towns in Holland; the films shown there read now like a record of avant-garde film-making at the time – works by Richter, Ruttman,

Eggeling, Clair, Dulac, Cavalcanti, Kirsanov, Turin, Dovzhenko, Eisenstein, Flaherty. Although Ivens' work at CAPI entailed making films for demonstration and sales purposes, his Filmliga activities pushed him in the direction of making films for his own experiments, as well as using CAPI resources for Filmliga needs – projection rooms, film stock, and personnel. Helen van Dongen, a major collaborator until 1940, was working as a secretary at CAPI at the time, dealing with international correspondence, and became the chief translator for the Filmliga, as well as becoming a camera operator and editor for Ivens when he started to make his own films. Apart from Ivens, she worked with Hans Richter (editing *Daily Life* in 1934) Joseph Losey (on *Petroleum*, 1939) and Robert Flaherty, (on *The Land* and *Louisiana Story*, to which she made major contributions). Her own films were *Russians at War* (1942), *News Review No. 2* (1944–45) and *Of Human Rights* (1949–50). When she married in 1950 she left film-making.

Ivens' first experiments are often compared to Ruttman's films, and although Ivens defined his own approach to film-making in contradistinction to Ruttman's, his own *Rain*, a study of the effect of rain on Amsterdam, can be read off against Ruttman's *Berlin*. Certainly his first experiment, *Zeedijk-Filmstudie* (1927), which he left unedited, contained a study in movement which refused Ruttman's appeal to uninterpretable abstraction.

1927: **Zeedijk-Filmstudie** (Filmstudy-Zeedijk) Holland 10 mins. silent b/w 35mm. No copy survives.

The film was shot in a bar run by Juffrouw Heyens, the mother of a sculptor friend. The bar was in the Zeedijk, part of Amsterdam's seamen's quarter. Ivens has described this first experiment and referred to its importance in being made in a real setting.

'My camera moved a lot – too much – which is the usual fault of the beginner. But some of the movement did help me to catch the atmosphere and gestures of the men standing at the bar. I remember one in particular: one of the drunks, who regularly became the King of Canada after his second bottle of gin, felt so fine and powerful that morning that he grabbed from the lamp the long brown ribbon of fly paper – coated with black, sticky flies – flung it round his neck with a magnificent swash-buckling gesture and, raising his bottle to his image in the mirror, toasted the health of the King of Canada. I managed to catch this in a pan shot, ending with a close-up of the king in the mirror. Back of the bar, in a sitting room with a direct view of the whole establishment, sat Juffrouw Heyens, with her rheumatic legs and her stiff knotted fingers, watching like a hawk from the security of her fireplace of blue Delft tiles . . . When I projected the printed footage I was surprised at how much of the quality of rough fun came across; and there was a certain pictorial accomplishment, giving some of the

12

intensity of old Dutch paintings of dark interiors. I didn't edit the material because I realised that this was a purely amateur achievement; but I had tested my talent, and the test had been conducted in a real setting and not in the abstract angles and curves of Ruttman.' ('Apprentice to Films', p.186)

The following year, whilst in Paris, Ivens attempted a study of Paris streets:

1928: **Etudes des mouvements** (Studies in Movement) France 7 mins. silent b/w 35mm.

Returning to Amsterdam, he began the film which first brought him European acclaim as an avant-garde film-maker.

1928: **De Brug** (The Bridge) Holland
Director   Joris Ivens
Camera   Joris Ivens
Editor   Joris Ivens
11 mins. silent b/w 35mm.
Première: 5 May 1928, Amsterdam Filmliga, Centraal Theatre, Amsterdam.

In making *The Bridge*, Ivens continued his investigations into rendering movement on the cinema screen. The idea for a subject came from an engineer who suggested that he look at the railway bridge over the Maas River in Rotterdam, which moved up and down to allow trains to pass over it and ships to pass beneath. In *The Camera and I*, Ivens recalled that:

'For me the bridge was a laboratory of movements, tones, shapes, contrasts, rhythms and the relations between all these . . . What I wanted was to find some general rules, laws of continuity of movement. Music had its rules and its grammar on tones, melody, and counterpoint . . . If anyone knew about the relation of motion on the screen he was keeping it to himself . . . I learnt from *The Bridge* that prolonged and creative observation is the only way to be sure of selecting, emphasising and squeezing everything possible out of the rich reality in front of you . . .' (p.26ff)

The contemporary importance of his film – aesthetically, as well as in its demonstration of what could be achieved on minimal resources – is indicated in a report from Belgium and Holland written for *Close Up* by Jean Lenauer:

'The public is not particularly interested in the difficulties which directors with limited resources have to overcome, and if I'm talking about this film, it is because I want to congratulate its maker, who has really produced a very original piece of work.
    'The theme of Joris Ivens' film is simply a railway bridge near Rotterdam, which is occasionally raised to allow ships to pass by.

13

'Yet really this film is a pure visual symphony, made with the highest technical understanding and an astonishing sureness of touch. As you watch the rare beauty of its composition, you feel impelled to give its maker the highest compliments. For in its composition the film reveals a new talent, Joris Ivens' talent, which uses no tricks, no subterfuges, and from which we can undoubtedly look forward, in the near future, to unsuspected levels of visual pleasure . . .' (*Close Up*, June 1928, pp.29–30)

Ivens was to have his confrontation with the demands of visual pleasure later, with *Borinage*, in 1933. In the meantime he turned his attention to a different problem: that of working with actors, using the human face as subject, rather than the exploration of machinery. *Breakers*, made in 1929, is unusual in Ivens' work– with *The First Years* (1949) it is a rare example of direct and sustained fiction film-making.

1929: **Branding** (Breakers) Holland

Directors	Joris Ivens, Mannus Franken
Script	Mannus Franken, from a story by Jef Last
Camera	Joris Ivens
Assistant Camera	John Fernhout
Editor	Joris Ivens
Music	
(to accompany projections)	Max Vredenburg

Cast
Jef Last: Unemployed Fisherman; Co Seiger: His Fiancée; Hein Block: Pawnbroker.
35 mins. silent b/w 35mm.
Première: 9 Feb 1929, Amsterdam Filmliga, Centraal Theatre, Amsterdam.

Shot in Katwyk, Holland, the film tells the story of a fisherman who, when unemployment comes, loses his fiancée to the advances of a pawnbroker– a man who has already taken most of his possessions. Having faced his despair he decides to leave his village for the sea.

'It took me more than one film to teach me to work with actors, but the important accomplishment for me in this film was some successes in photographic ingenuity. In order to film the movement of the sea and the surf in a dramatic, subjective way, I constructed a rubber sack with a glass front to contain my head and arms and camera. This enabled me to shoot while breakers rolled over my camera and myself, producing shots of sea movement of a violent quality that nobody had seen before on the screen.
'Mannus Franken did much of the direction for me. It was good training to work with faces and human features and with reactions so soon after the mechanised movements on *The Bridge*. Creating certain moods of a fishing community in a minimum of shots was a challenging problem for a young film-maker: a lone dog in an empty street; a sleepy pan-shot along the

straight lines of the tiny roofs; a single child in a spotless court; a line of dignified fishermen walking stiffly in their black Sunday clothes against the white austere architecture of the village church. For us *Breakers* was a good film, although I remember we thought the Filmliga audiences didn't like it because they had become a bit snobbish.' (*The Camera and I*, p.34)

In making *Breakers* Ivens was joined for the first time by John Fernhout (later known as Ferno), then just fourteen, who became a member of the Ivens team, notably in Spain and China, working on war films. He is also a documentarist in his own right.

It was in 1929, too, that Ivens made his second major experimental film, *Rain*.

1929: **Regan** (Rain) Holland
Director   Joris Ivens
Script   Joris Ivens and Mannus Franken
Camera   Joris Ivens
Editor   Joris Ivens, with assistance from Mannus Franken
12 mins. silent b/w 35mm.
A sound version was prepared in 1932 by Helen van Dongen with music by Lou Lichtveld.

A glimpse of one particular way of placing Ivens' work is provided by Bela Balazs, the Hungarian critic and film-maker, who, whilst politically critical of the director's stance, links his discussions of *Rain* and *Bridge* to an analysis of formalism and of the 'absolute' film which seeks to liberate film form from the limits of 'literariness':

'The Dutch film-maker Joris Ivens, one of the greatest artists of pictorial poetry, no longer wanted to show objective realities to the spectator. His famous impressionist films, *Rain* and *The Bridge,* do not represent either objects or facts which we might have possibly seen in their actual being . . . the rain-pictures of Ivens could not be seen by anyone else in any rain; at most he could recognise them after seeing the Ivens pictures and after his eyes had been sufficiently trained by them. Ivens' moods and impressions dematerialise their theme. Who could find the atmosphere of Claude Monet's paintings in actual nature? They do not exist outside those paintings, outside the experience which Monet painted into his work. Nor can one imagine behind Ivens' film pictures objects that exist independently of these pictures. This is the "absolute" film.

'The rain we see in the Ivens film is not one particular rain which fell somewhere, some time. These visual impressions are not bound into unity by any conception of time and space. With subtle sensitivity he has captured, not what rain really is, but what it looks like when a soft spring rain drips off leaves, the surface of a pond gets gooseflesh from the rain, a solitary raindrop hesitatingly gropes its way down a window-pane, or the wet pavement reflects the life of a city. We get a hundred visual impressions, but never the things themselves; nor do these interest us in such films. All we want to see are the individual, intimate, surprising optical effects. Not the things but these their pictures constitute our experience and we do not think of any objects behind such pictures, which are images, not reproductions.

'Even when Ivens shows a bridge and tells us that it is the great railway bridge at Rotterdam, the huge iron structure dissolves into an immaterial picture of a hundred angles. The mere fact that one can see this one Rotterdam bridge on such a multitude of pictures almost robs it of its reality. It seems not a utilitarian bit of engineering but a series of strange optical effects, visual variations on a theme, and one can scarcely believe that a goods train could possibly pass over it. Every set-up has a different physiognomy, a different character, but none of them has anything whatever to do with either the purpose of the bridge or its architectural qualities.' (Bela Balazs, *Theory of the Film*, pp.175–176, Dennis Dobson, London 1952)

Unfinished projects for that year consisted of two attempts to achieve identification between film-maker, camera and spectator via the development of a 'subjective' camera.

1929: **Schaatsenrijden** (Skating) Holland
8 mins. silent b/w 35mm.

'I used my subjective handcamera and filmed my own feet as they moved over the ice.' (*The Camera and I*, p.41)

1929: **Ik-Film** (I Film) Holland
10 mins. silent b/w 35mm.

This 'subject' camera was, in Helen van Dongen's words:

'A platform with concentric wheels on which a kinamo was mounted. The camera took the place of the human eye, theoretically at any rate, and "walked" like a man. This experiment was called the *Ik-Film*. But since a camera has a fixed lens without the equilibrium and compensation of human vision, I will leave the results to your imagination.' (Helen van Dongen, *Joris Ivens*, Festschrift der Staatlichen Film Archiv der DDR, Berlin, 1963)

After the success of *Bridge* and *Rain*, Ivens found himself approached to make commercial films and accepted three commissions over the next two years: first from the Dutch Building Workers Union (ANB – Algemene Nederlandsche Bowarbeidersbond) to make a recruitment film to celebrate their 25th anniversary – *Wij Bouwen* (We are Building) – next from Philips

Engineering of Eindhoven, to make a publicity film (*Philips Radio*) and then from the International Committee of Creosote Manufacturers, to make another publicity film (*Creosote*). On the basis of the first commission a film production unit was set up within CAPI, and making these three films was Ivens' first experience of working with sponsors – although of different kinds.

1929: **Wij Bouwen** (We are Building) Holland
Production	CAPI-Amsterdam, with ANB
Director	Joris Ivens
Script	Joris Ivens, in collaboration with ANB
Camera	Joris Ivens
Editor	Joris Ivens
Musical accompaniment	Hugo de Groot

110 mins. silent b/w 35mm.
Premiè: AMVJ (General Social Youth Assn., Amsterdam, 1929.

In gathering material for *We are Building*, Ivens shot footage of the many different types of work members of the union performed, with emphasis on the craft aspect. One of these projects – the draining of the Zuiderzee, became the subject of a short film *Zuiderzee*. Filming of the project continued until 1933, and different versions were made. A final version, called *New Earth*, was completed in 1934. Other short films were also made on the basis of footage shot during the making of *We are Building*. In all, collaboration with the Building Workers Union produced six other films apart from *We are Building*.

1929: **Heien** (Pile Driving) Holland
10 mins. silent b/w. Musical accompaniment written by Lou Lichtveld.

'The city of Amsterdam is built on swampy ground. No new building can be erected until heavy wooden piles have been driven down through the mud into solid ground. These are the building's foundations. I went to extremes to obtain the full physical effect of the rhythmic powerful pounding. I even had myself tied to the driving hammer to get a little closer to the sensation of the actual impact . . .' (*The Camera and I*, p.45)

1929: **Nieuwe Architectuur** (New Architecture) Holland
5 mins. silent b/w 35mm.

'*New Architecture* was to show what had already been accomplished in modern Dutch architecture, already internationally famous for its simplicity and imaginative functionalism . . . This film was made as much for the young Dutch architects, who were amongst the most ardent Filmliga members, as it was for the union menbers.' (*The Camera and I*, p.45)

1929: **Caissonbouw Rotterdam** Holland
6 mins. silent b/w 35mm.
No copy survives.

1929: **Zuid Limburg** (South Limburg) Holland
6 mins. silent b/w 35mm.
No copy survives.

1929: **Jeugddag** (Day of Youth) Holland
Directors   Wim Bon, Jan Hin
Editors   Joris Ivens, Wim Bon
35 mins. silent b/w 35mm.

A film report of a 'youth day' organised by the Building Workers Union.
Only a few sequences survive.

1930: **Zuiderzee** Holland
Producer   CAPI-Amsterdam
Director   Joris Ivens
Script   Joris Ivens
Camera   Joris Ivens, John Fernhout, Joop Huisken,
                                     Helen van Dongen, Eli Lotar
Editor   Helen van Dongen
45 mins. silent b/w 35mm.

It was also in 1929 that Ivens was invited to make his first visit to the Soviet
Union, as the result of a personal invitation from Pudovkin. Like other film
societies, the Filmliga had been extremely important for the introduction
and distribution of films from the new Soviet cinema within Europe. It was
Filmliga practice, too, to invite directors to talk about their films, and
although the Dutch authorities had made restrictive conditions about
duration of visits and types of audience, Pudovkin had visited Amsterdam
and the Filmliga in January 1929. Ivens' own editing technique had been
influenced by shot-by-shot breakdowns of some Russian films – *Potemkin*
and *Arsenal* amongst them. The Russian cinema was looked at very much as
an alternative to the dominant commercial cinema in the West – its vitality
held out a hope and a promise. The showing of Russian films, too, raised
sharply the issues of internal censorship.

Zuiderzee was greeted by Pudovkin as a 'leap forward'. Since Ivens was
the first foreign director to be invited to make a film in the Soviet Union,
and Helen van Dongen, its editor, later worked in the Moscow Academy of
Cinematography (1934–36) lecturing on editing as well as taking courses,
Pudovkin's reaction to *Zuiderzee* can help to illuminate the values which this
Russian director was bringing to Ivens' work.

'I was extremely surprised and happy that after his two previous rather
formalist film essays, *Rain* and *Bridge*, Ivens' film *Zuiderzee* treats the

19

draining of the Zuiderzee after the manner of a reportage. What has happened? All the defects which struck me in Ivens' first work have vanished. With this film he has made not just a step, but a leap forward. The unsure and troubled montage of *Bridge* and *Rain*, which corresponded to an uncertain and restless conception of the world, has been replaced by a tranquil, clear, definite rhythm. How can one explain this change in Ivens? To begin with he has overcome his earlier principles, which were those of an uncertain aesthetic, and he has passed to the cinematographic creation of "living realities". This "passage" is the result of the union between an artist and the organisation of the revolutionary workers movement in Holland. Ivens' camera no longer slides superficially over life's phenomena. He has chosen as a theme the immense work of draining the sea bed, the filling in of the Zuiderzee, a technical labour of the working class, which affirms the future of the proletariat and human labour. Here Ivens shows himself not as a director – camera operator who passes at the side of the essential problems of life today, but as a man who thinks concretely.

'Further, this is not merely an artist working with his subject and making it submit to his programme; it is the subject which inevitably reverberates back on to the artist, during the process of work, and which makes him achieve awareness. This is what happened in *Zuiderzee*. Ivens has chosen human labour as a theme, and this labour has submitted him to its laws: it dictates to him its precise and convincing rhythms, it gives the film's montage its clarity and precision. It gives birth to what one calls "artistic truth", that is to say, an inherent organic logic which creates the unity and power of conviction of artistic work and which makes art dependent on living reality . . . Here Ivens is not just in contact with the iron of machinery (as in *Bridge*) or with men and water (as in *Rain*). In the dynamic of common work, lived through and filmed by Ivens, everything has suddenly come alive. People no longer "set in motion" their everyday dress (as in *Rain*). They concentrate all their forces in making a new piece of land rise from the bottom of the sea'. (Vsevolod Pudovkin, 'Joris Ivens', *Rote Fahne*, 17, March 1931)

Pudovkin, in welcoming Ivens' passage from formalism to 'living themes', and in positing this change as a result of working with a working-class organisation, is picking up and using some contemporary threads of internal political and cultural debate in the Soviet Union. The model which he sets up has often been repeated in discussion of Ivens' work – according to some (for example, Catherine Grenier, 'Joris Ivens: social realist versus lyric poet', *Sight and Sound*, Spring 1958), there are two Ivens styles, or rather a tension between two modes of film-making in Ivens' work – the poetic, impressionistic cameraman, and the realist documentarist.

Given this emphasis, it is perhaps important to point out the development of technique in *Zuiderzee*. Particularly in the filming of the closing of the dyke, where different cameras were set up to identify with the different

'actors' involved – the land, the sea, and the crane – there can be traced a continuing interest in the problem of the 'subjective' camera, although it is here transposed on to other elements than the human eye.

During 1929–30 Ivens was involved with the production of other short films for working-class organisations in Holland. No copies surivive of any of these shorts:

1929: **NVV Congress** Holland
Camera   Joris Ivens
Editor   Joris Ivens
30 mins. silent b/w 35mm.

Report on the 1929 Congress of the Dutch Federation of Trades Unions (NVV).

1929: **Arm Drenthe** Holland
Producer   Leo van Lakerveld for the VVVC (Vereniging
                                  Voor Volks Cultuur – Association for
                                    Popular Culture)
Camera   Joris Ivens
15 mins. silent b/w 35mm.
Première: 1 March 1929, Cinema Royal, Amsterdam.

Documentary about the life of workers in Drenthe.

21

1930: **De Tribune Film; Breken en Bouwen** Holland
Producer   Leo van Lakerveld
Camera   Joris Ivens
Editor   Joris Ivens
20 mins. silent b/w 35mm.
Première: Tuschinski Theatre, Amsterdam, 26 November 1930.

Publicity film for *Tribune*, the daily paper of the Dutch Communist Party.

Ivens was also, during 1929, film programmer for the Association for Popular Culture (vvvc), and on his return from the Soviet Union helped to edit film journals for them, none of which survive.

1930: **Film Notities uit de Sovjet-Unie** (News from the Soviet Union) Holland
20 mins. silent b/w 35mm.
Première: Tuschinski Theatre, Amsterdam, 16 November 1930.

1930: **Demostratie van Proletarische Solidariteit** (Demonstration of Proletarian Solidarity) Holland
Producer   Leo van Lakerveld
Editor   Joris Ivens
20 mins. silent b/w 35mm.
Première: Tuschinski Theatre, 1930.

His main cinematic concern in this year, however, was the production of *Philips Radio*, a publicity film about the work of the Eindhoven factory which produced radio sets. The only constraint Philips put on the film was that everything had to be shot *inside* the factory. Nothing could therefore be shown of the workers' home conditions.

 Helen van Dongen, who had been studying sound recording and soundtrack editing in Paris at the Tobis Klangfilm Studios and at the UFA studios in Berlin, was once more a part of the production unit and *Philips Radio* is an early example of the sound technique she developed. John Fernhout worked on camera once more. *Philips Radio* is one of the first examples of a commercially sponsored industrial documentary; its success encouraged Philips to expand their use of film for public relations purposes, their subsequent productions including Hans Richter's *Radio Europa*.

1931: **Philips Radio** (French title: *Symphonie industrielle*) Holland
Production: CAPI-Amsterdam, in collaboration
         with Philips, Eindhoven
Director   Joris Ivens
Script   Joris Ivens
Camera   Joris Ivens, John Fernhout, Mark Kolthouf
Editors   Joris Ivens, Helen van Dongen
Music   Lou Lichtveld
36 mins. sound b/w 35mm.

Ivens' achievement with *Philips Radio* was to construct, in a sense, a documentary *Modern Times*. Like Chaplin's film, *Philips Radio* criticises the domination of the machine in the capitalist organisation of the labour process. The laboratory work and recording were carried out in the Tobis Klangfilm Studios in Paris, at the same time as René Clair was beginning work on *A nous la liberté*. As part of preparation for this film, which uses a modern factory setting, Clair showed *Philips Radio* to his crew. The film critic and theatre director Léon Moussinac, in a contemporary review, contrasted *Philips Radio* (under its French title) with Ruttman's *Mélodie du monde*.

'They are both films made for publicity purposes: the first (*Mélodie du monde*) for a large German navigation company, the second (*Symphonie industrielle*) for the most important European factory producing electric lamps and radio receivers.

They both manage (in different ways, certainly, but ways which show how intelligence can cheat obstacles and succeed against all one's expectations) to present us with complete films, full of meaning, with a strong social emphasis, in spite of their imposed advertising function.

'*Mélodie du monde* is a touching film, and I will not repeat here the reasons I have already given for admiring it. *Symphonie industrielle* is dramatic. In strong and striking images, with a determined rhythm, it raises the spectre of the physical and moral ruin which threatens those workers who are the victims of capitalist rationalisation and those workers whom the machine has not yet freed from certain forms of labour.

'Here we have a "model" factory, that is to say, one where everything is co-ordinated – machinery, personnel, organisation – so that industrial efficiency is raised to the highest level, and so that production reaches that frontier of intensity beyond which only catastrophe can follow. Machines and muscles are held at work for shifts which use, ruin and disorganise the poor human mechanism, in a flow which does not allow of failure or of clumsy gestures, which ties the worker to his task and, instead of liberating the worker from the superfluous element of his labour, draws from him a productive capacity whose accelerated rhythm and unorganised distribution can only swell the owner's profits until crisis point is reached.

'We also see the tragic face of a science which has not yet discovered mechanical methods of replacing all forms of old-fashioned glass-blowing. So here are men – young men, because they die young in this trade – who empty their lungs in unison so as to make giant neon bulbs for advertising and powerful arc-lamps. Their cheeks are hideously deformed, their faces are wrinkled, and the film hints, via a play on black and white, at how much illness wears away their over-extended bodies . . . To a certain extent, as well as being an accomplished piece of cinema, *Symphonie industrielle* is an act of accusation against the present economic system. That is why we can remain indifferent to the advertising cause it serves (although not very effectively) and why we would also hope for the film to be widely shown in public cinemas and also in workers' cinemas, where its message would be easily picked up.' (Léon Moussinac, *L'Humanité*, 1931)

The creosote manufacturers approached Ivens almost as soon as *Philips Radio* was completed. Jean Dreville, the French cameraman, joined the team, and footage was shot on location in Belgium, Holland, Poland, Germany and France.

1931: **Creosoot** (Creosote) Holland
Producer   CAPI-Amsterdam, in collaboration with the International Committee of Creosote Manufacturers
Director   Joris Ivens
Camera   Jean Dreville, Eli Lotar, John Fernhout
Script   Joris Ivens
Editor   Joris Ivens
Animated sequences by UFA-Kulutrabteilung, Berlin.
80 mins. silent b/w 35mm.

Both *Philips Radio* and *Creosote* were commercially successful for CAPI. After completing *Creosote* Ivens made one of the most important political and artistic decisions of his film career and left Holland to make a film in the Soviet Union, the first foreign director to do so.

With his departure for the Soviet Union, Ivens was beginning a life as an international film director which would only permit him to make two further films using Holland as a base – *New Earth* in 1934, and *Rotterdam-Europort* in 1966. So it is interesting to find in Helen van Dongen's memoir of Joris Ivens a description of what was being (albeit unknowingly) left behind. Here she describes his flat in Het Singel, Amsterdam, and some of the production techniques and conditions of the Filmliga period:

'Another centre of activity, about two blocks away from the projection room at CAPI, was an old loft building on Het Singel, one of the major canals that encircled the old city of Amsterdam. Ivens occupied the top two floors. By courtesy of the press this real bohemian garret was known as "Joris Ivens' Studio". To the habitues and students it was simply "Het Singel". The lower of the two top floors was divided in half. The front half was Ivens' "home", the back half contained the beginnings of a film library: international weekly or monthly magazines and a number of scientific books. In addition it served as an overflow centre for the students, all sorts of film-experiments or just people . . .

'The top floor was just one small room, maybe about 50 feet long. At the far end a small part was blocked off and made into a developing laboratory. The long walls on either side were interrupted by many windows, furnishing convenient "back-light" to view film strips by hand. On one side

24

was the long, plain wooden table, with the reminders and the film viewing head and piles and piles of film cans with a little space left over for film-splicing. This was done by wetting the end with the tongue, scraping off the emulsion with a piece of glass, putting a little cement on it and then quickly putting the other end, glossy side down, as straight as possible, on the first piece, pushing down with the thumb to hold it together. After about thirty seconds one released the splice and pulled carefully. If it did not hold you started all over again.

'On the opposite side of the table were hung long, horizontal rods, with headless nails about every 3cm. This was our "montage room". Whole film sequences in their preliminary, theoretical order according to content, could be hung out there. One began by breaking down the film into single shots and sorting them, each shot in full length, each strip hanging from the nail by the sprocket-hole. Spacing them far enough from each other, new-found shots could be inserted or the order changed. Only after one was theoretically satisfied with the progression of the separate shots would the actual cutting of the film begin, at first roughly, according to movement and length, gradually more and more precisely. Naturally the theoretical order at first decided on would have to be changed. One regrouped, discarded more shots and added new scenes the more the montage reached its ultimate form.

'In this room on Het Singel were edited such films as *The Bridge, Rain, Zuiderzee* and *We are Building,* all Ivens' films, as well as *Creosote,* edited by Jean Dreville, or *Boek* by Willem Bon, and many others. Jan Hin, Eisenstein, Cavalcanti, Man Ray, and many others could be found here at one time or another . . .

'The top floor of Het Singel was the real hub of the film-producing wheel where most of the original Filmliga members who eventually formed the nucleus of the avant-garde film makers in Holland could be found at one time or another. In the midst of it Joris Ivens, the man with a limitless energy and a passion for film, was ever present. Then, gradually, came the time when film-making became more organised and, still later, when sound was added to film. With the perfection and increasing complexity of technique Het Singel became inadequate for professional production and we had to move to other countries where the studio facilities were more advanced. Gradually, too, came the time when Ivens would be on the go: to Belgium for *Borinage* or to Russia for *Song of Heroes.'*

3 Left Politics and Cinema I: 1932-37

When Ivens arrived in Moscow, in 1932, the Soviet Union was in the throes of the First Five Year Plan, conceived as a first push to make the Soviet Union self-sufficient industrially and agriculturally. Mezhrabpom, the studio with which Ivens worked, suggested to Ivens a subject similar to

Zuiderzee – the draining of swamps in the Caucasus as a basis for citrus fruit production. Ivens, however, chose instead as a location and subject the Ural-Kuznetz project, started in 1930, whose aim was to link the iron ore of the Urals with the coking coal of Central Sibera – one thousand miles away. This project entailed a huge capital investment and the thinking behind it was partially military-strategic. After the Russian Revolution, during the German advance and the War of Intervention which followed (1918–22), the area under Bolshevik control had been cut off from the main areas of industrial production, situated as they were towards the Western frontiers of Russia. The aim of the Ural-Kuznetz project was to create a metallurgical base in the rear, in case of future war. Although the project was extremely expensive, it paid off in industrial and military terms during the Second World War.

The central location in the Urals was Magnitogorsk, where blast furnaces were being built next to what had recently been a small khirgiz village, in order to utilise the iron ore from the magnetic mountain of Magitnaya; in Siberia the location was Kuznetz. The focus of the film is on the building of a blast furnace by young workers – to be called *Komsomolskaya* after the *Komsomol*, the Young Communist League. Hence one of the film's titles – *Komsomol*. Production was geared to coincide with the completion of the first Five Year Plan, and the film was one of ten shown to celebrate its completion.

1931: **Pesn o Gerojach** (Komsomol, or Song of Heroes) USSR
Producer   Mezhrabpom-Film, Moscow
Director   Joris Ivens
Script   I. Skliut
Camera   Alexander Shelenkov
Editor   Joris Ivens
Music   Hanns Eisler
Production Adviser   Andreyev
Sound Engineer   Nikitin
Production Assistant   Herbert Marshall
50 mins. sound b/w 35mm.
Première: Moscow, October 1932.

Komsomol is the first film within which Ivens uses the story of an individual as a narrative device – a device also used in *Spanish Earth* and *The First Years*. It is also the first film in which he uses the much-debated technique of re-enactment, that is, the re-staging of events, usually chosen for their emotional significance within the meanings the films construct, so as to allow maximum flexibility for the camera. It is this technique which establishes a porous frontier between documentary and fictional forms, and it is Ivens' openness about its use which has helped to stimulate the debate.

There are two re-enacted scenes in *Komsomol*. In one, young workers carrying torches arrive in trucks to put in extra hours of work at night. Such

26

events did happen, but the one recorded in the film was staged and directed for maximum cinematic impact. In the other, Afanaseyev, the young khirgiz worker, signs on for work on the building site. This scene was recreated in a Moscow studio, and is therefore in synch. This use of re-enactment led to debate with Vertov's group (from the other side, Ivens was criticised for not going into sufficient psychological depth with Afanaseyev, and therefore, in a sense, not being fictional enough). The re-creation of the employment office was certainly in part determined by the technical problems posed by the location and the available equipment. Dziga Vertov himself used re-enactment in *Three Songs for Lenin*, which he directed for Mezhrabpom in 1934. In an article he drafted but never published on the need for better facilities, he wrote, *a propos* this experience, that:

'The first important obstacle we ran up against was the impossibility of synchronising sound and shot, whatever the subject. The equipment at Mezhrabpom-Film's disposal needed a 3-phase electricity supply to be brought to the location. It was technically impossible to film people in a village, in their fields, in their natural *milieu* and to follow their behaviour. We did not immediately consider this a primordial obstacle, but in all our memoranda we argued that it was essential to create mobile equipment which would allow us to film in synch. on every location and at every moment. In the meantime, in the standard conditions of current cinema production, we have been able to resolve these problems in words only, in the form of promises and resolutions. In fact we have gained nothing except promises whose realisation is put off from today to tomorrow – "tomorrow" not being taken in its definite but in its indefinite meaning. It is a tomorrow which we approach at the same speed as do two parallel lines.' (Dziga Vertov, *Articles, Journaux, Projets*, tr. and ed. by Sylviane Mossé and Andrée Robel, Collection 10:18, *Cahiers du Cinéma*, Paris 1972, pp.185–6)

However, it would be misleading to give the impression that Ivens chose re-enactment only for technical reasons. In *The Camera and I* he recalled that: 'I could not agree with the Vertov approach to this big question of documentary truth . . . The distinction between letting the event dominate the filming and the attempt to film an event with maximum expressiveness is the difference between orthodox documentary (which today is represented by the newsreel) and the newer, broader form of documentary film.' (p.76)

On his return to Amsterdam, Ivens was invited by the Belgian film-maker Henri Storck to make a film with him in the Borinage, the main coal-producing region of Belgium.

1933: **Misère au Borinage** (Borinage) Belgium

Producer	EPI (Education par l'Image) – Club de l'Ecran, Brussels
Directors	Joris Ivens, Henri Storck

Script	Joris Ivens, Henri Storck
Camera	Joris Ivens, Henri Storck, François Rents
Editors	Joris Ivens, Henri Storck

34 mins. silent b/w 35mm.
Première: Brussels, 6 March 1934.
Later versions
1934: Russian Version

Producer	Mezhrabpom-Film, Moscow
Editors	Jay Leyda, Helen van Dongen
Music	Hans Hanska
Commentary	I Skliut

1960: Sound Version
Prepared by Henri Storck

Commentary	André Thirifays

'During the summer of 1933 the Club de l'Ecran in Brussels, an important left-wing cinema club run by Pierre Vermeylen and André Thirifays, suggested that I make a film report on the social consequences of the revolutionary miners strike in the Borinage which had taken place in 1932. I immediately thought of asking Joris Ivens if he would make the film with me. He had just returned to Amsterdam from the USSR after finishing his film on the Komsomol. Ivens accepted my offer and we left for the Borinage to begin our investigation. The miners' situation shocked and revolted us. We stopped thinking about the cinema and how to frame shots and instead became dominated by the irrepressible need to produce images as stark, bare, and sincere as possible to fit the cruel facts reality had thrown at us. Any attempt at aestheticism seemed indecent. Our camera had to carry a cry of revolt.

'The miners understood that our enterprise was an honest one; they trusted us and helped us unreservedly, allowing us to go into their homes and film their atrocious poverty. We ourselves were not rich, Vermeylen, Thirifays and some other friends – mainly left intellectuals – had raised about ten thousand francs to pay for film-stock, processing, and a few days work from the excellent Belgian cameraman François Rents. Most of the images were filmed by Ivens and myself using our own Kinamos.

'We filmed during September 1933. We could not use arc-lamps – the workers were too poor to pay their electricity bills, so the supply had been cut off – but used oil lamps instead. Their light and heat attracted clouds of slimy insects which surged from the walls of the houses and from behind the wallpaper.

'The police, alerted by the management of the mine companies, were at our heels every day. They could not prevent me, a Belgian, from filming freely in my own country: then, as now, no permission to film was needed; but Ivens was a suspect foreigner because of his political ideas: it was known that he had just returned from the USSR and frequented communist circles. So he often had to hide, spending the night with workers who gave him shelter. He had to avoid being caught with his camera in his hand, otherwise there would be delicate explanations to the police and the danger of expulsion from Belgium. This climate of semi-clandestinity gave filming the flavour of adventure and made us feel even more solidarity with the savage struggle which some organised groups of workers were conducting . . . Our film did not lie, and nor did it exaggerate. From that reality we chose the aspects with most meaning. Above all we wanted to shout our indignation by using the starkest images possible, images of an abominable reality we had seen and lived through with the miners and their families . . . We were doing something of which the orthodoxy of right and left would disapprove, but we were forced to do it and felt happy to do it . . .' (Henri Storck, in *Joris Ivens, 50 ans de cinéma*, Jean-Loup Passek, Paris 1979)

It is interesting to look at *Borinage* in relation to Ivens' most recent experiences. His experience in Belgium provided an opportunity to verify a developing theoretical and political position. The historical lens of class struggle is one of the instruments used in the film's construction. Conditions in the Borinage are explained by reference to the anarchy of the economic system and the brutality of the forces which sustain it, rather than as an accident of history which investment in welfare can correct. At the beginning and end of the film a juxtaposition of images links the theme of poverty in the midst of plenty to crises of over-production, demonstrates the severity of punishment meted out to those who oppose such a state of affairs, and refers, via the final image of Lenin, to the Russian Revolution as an exemplary route out of such crises. In the Russian version the conditions of Belgian miners are compared, negatively, to those of Russian miners.

Ivens also uses his recently developed technique of re-enactment. There are three examples of this: a scene where workers play cards in the street because meetings have been banned, then run across to form an impromptu meeting; a scene where workers prevent an eviction order from being served; a scene of a demonstration in Wasmes to commemorate the death of Karl Marx. And although the material is shot after the strike the film uses newspaper cuttings and other material to attempt to indicate the course and main elements of the strike of 1932 – in that sense the whole film is an attempt at reconstruction.

Borinage also moves in the direction of a new aesthetics, an accusatory aesthetics which refuses the polish and immediate visual appeal of Ivens' early work. Its appeal is to the recognition of a suffering which is appalling because it is wasteful and unnecessary, and emphasis is laid on the production and selection of images which can convey the waste. It is the same approach which Ivens adopts later, in Vietnam, when he stops his camera before the shot reaches palm trees, so as not to summon up romantic colonial associations. But this different aesthetics marked a break with an avant-garde which desired visual pleasure above all things, and read from its apparent absence an absence of 'art'. And *Borinage*, too, emerged into a world where international crises were intensifying political choices and defining new boundaries. With *Borinage* Ivens' work moved out of the opposition art/commerce of the Filmliga years and into the opposition art/politics.

The other major problem faced by the Filmliga – censorship – remained an issue, however, for *Borinage*. The film was refused general release and could only be shown in film-clubs. The problems of achieving general release and commercial distribution have remained problems throughout Ivens' career. He has been called, with some justification, the most censored film-maker in the world.

Returning to Holland, Ivens' next film, *New Earth*, pursued the theme of an international capitalist crisis of over-production.

1934: **Nieuwe Gronden** (New Earth) Holland

Producer	CAPI-Amsterdam
Director	Joris Ivens
Script	Joris Ivens
Camera	Joris Ivens, Joop Huisken, John Fernhout, Helen van Dongen
Editors	Helen van Dongen, Joris Ivens
Music	Hanns Eisler
Ballad	Julian Arendt & Ernst Busch, sung by Ernst Busch in the German version, Jan van den Broek in the Dutch
Sound editing	Helen van Dongen
Commentary	Written and spoken by Joris Ivens

New Earth includes material shot for *Zuiderzee* and *We are Building*. In an interview recorded in 1976, Helen van Dongen reflected on the experience of making *New Earth* and of seeing it after 30 years:

'*Was* New Earth *the first film in which you were working with stock footage as well as material you and your crew had shot?*

'Yes. But actually there are very few stock shots. Some of the scenes which look like stock footage were shot by us in re-enactment. We bought a few sacks of wheat and burned it and filmed that. The milk being thrown away, yes that is stock footage, and so are the scenes of the stock exchange crash.

'There are several versions of *New Earth*. The one now ending with the economic crash, accompanied by Hanns Eisler's song, was not planned like that originally. It grew out of the economic-political situation in Holland and the rest of the world . . .

'When I saw *New Earth* about two years ago I remembered how beautiful the film *could* be when one takes enough time to develop the theme of the dyke building and show the people who do the building. Then if, after sufficient time, you are told that they are now all unemployed, you have more compassion. Instead, in its present form, all the aspects of the dyke building are reduced to their essentials; all of a sudden the dam is closed and then, whammy, comes the shouting voice telling you that 20,000 workers after so many years of labour are now unemployed. The intention was to jar you into reality. In a way it does, but I think it could have been done better and with a more lasting effect by not using the sledge-hammer method. I know why it was done this way and I worked on it myself, but I do not think any longer that this was the right way of doing it, artistically. I can think of different ways which would have been more effective. It was in the beginning of using film as a political weapon, though, and as such it served probably a very good purpose'. ('Helen van Dongen: An Interview', Ben Achtenberg, *Film Quarterly,* Winter 1976)

The contemporary impact of *New Earth* can be gauged from this account in *New Movies,* the American National Board of Review magazine, which printed an appreciation of Ivens' work shortly after he first arrived in America:

'*New Earth*, the latest film, is also the best. The best technically and the most eloquent. What it says is implicit in what it shows – and what it says is profound and searching. It is a record of the making of new farmland for Holland by dyking off some of the Zyder Zee, and after the long years of labour, the growing of the first wheat crops. It is a remarkable picture of all the steps of the work, multitudinous in detail but single and clear in outline – men with their hands, their ships, their tools, their machines, driving back the sea till the triumphant climax when the last gap is filled, and the land is won. Man has conquered nature. Then more work, to make the land tillable and plant the grain and grow it. Till harvest time; then the crashing of markets, the tumbling to pieces of world distribution; though millions are starving in other parts of the earth the grain in these hard-won fields is not worth harvesting – it cannot be sold. So fire is set to it, or it is dumped over the wall into the sea. Man is defeated by the foolish ways of his fellow man.

'On the surface this is all just something that happened. And an amazing surface it is. Full of energy and vitality, rich in little observations that keep you constantly aware that the men are men, men who work and rest from work, who eat and have families – who conquer the sea, and then find it hardly worth having done. Beneath the surface of what happened at one particular place at one particular time runs the deeper, longer story of the struggle of man in the world, and his victories and defeats. At the end of the film comes a song, which may or may not point up a moral – it is in Dutch, so an American does not know. But no pointing up of a moral is needed – the perfection of the picture as a cinematic creation is in its saying what it has to say, completely and unmistakably, in its own medium of the camera, without the slightest need of comment or explanation.' (J. S. Hamilton, 'Joris Ivens' in *New Movies*, May 1936, p.10)

New Earth has also been a much-censored film. In many countries the last reel, which deals with the crisis, was cut and no full-length version exists in England.

After *New Earth* the team which worked on it was dispersed, although they were to work together again. Hanns Eisler, who had incorporated themes from *Kuhle Wampe* (1932) into the score of *New Earth*, had left Germany in 1933 with the Fascist rise to power there. He was to go to America from Europe in 1939, where he composed the score for *The Four Hundred Million* (1939). John Fernhout made his first documentary, *Easter Island*, in 1934, in collaboration with Henri Storck, and changed his name to Ferno. Joris Ivens and Helen van Dongen travelled to Moscow, where they worked with Gustav von Wagenheim, a German emigrant, on a film about the Reichstag fire, *Borza* (The Struggle). The Reichstag, the German Parliament, was set alight on 27 February 1933, six days before a general election. The arson was attributed to communists, and the following day all communist deputies were arrested and in the following days hundreds of 'marxists' – communists and social-democrats – were imprisoned. The elections then showed a fascist victory, after which the full range of fascist policies, including persecution of Jews, was put into effect. The suspicion was that the Reichstag fire was a fascist provocation, and the aim of this film was to explore the circumstances surrounding the fire. Material included filmed interviews with Georgi Dimitrov, the Bulgarian communist who was accused, and found not guilty, of participation in a plot to start the fire. Ivens collaborated on an initial script for *Borza*, whilst Helen van Dongen was the film's editor and assistant producer. In 1936 they both left Russia for the USA, Helen van Dongen travelling to Hollywood to study American production techniques.

Ivens had been invited to the USA by the New York Film Alliance, to show his films and lecture on them. But it was to be the war in Spain which was the next object of his film-making.

The Spanish Civil War broke out in July 1936, when General Franco led an expedition from the Canary Islands against the Republican Government of Spain. Franco's forces rapidly dominated North Central Spain, except for the Northern strip of the Asturias and the Basque country, establishing their base at Burgos. The government controlled the East (Catalonia and part of Aragon) and South Central Spain, including Madrid. South Western Spain was controlled by Franco's forces.

Together with John Dos Passos, the American writer, Helen van Dongen began work in 1936 on a compilation film, *Spain in Flames*, using newsreel footage, but the pro-Francoist slant of this material made the project of a documentary filmed on the spot in government areas seem imperative. On the initiative of Archibald MacLeish, a group of writers – Herman Shumlin (who acted as producer), Lillian Hellman and Dorothy Parker set up a production company, Contemporary Historians Inc., and raised three thousand dollars immediately with which to send Ivens to Spain and begin shooting. The US climate at that time, the years of Roosevelt's Presidency and the New Deal, was sympathetic to left-wing opinion, but in the post-war backlash against the New Deal and the period of the Un-American Activities Committee, those who supported the making of *Spanish Earth* and the later *400 Million* thereby won for themselves the peculiar HUAC appellation of 'premature anti-fascist'.

Ivens travelled to Madrid via Valencia with John Ferno, then based in Paris, who shot eighty per cent of the footage in Spain, and they were later joined by Dos Passos. After Dos Passos left the crew, Ernest Hemingway, the war correspondent for the North American News Alliance, joined it. Most of the film was shot in Fuentaduena, a village on the river Tagus, near the central front, whose survival was bound up with the defence of Madrid. Ivens' *Spanish Earth* has since taken its place, with Malraux's *L'Espoir* and Esther Shub's *Spain* (shot by Roman Karmen in Spain at the same time as the making of *Spanish Earth*) as a major film of the Spanish Civil War. Its first showing in Spain took place in 1977, forty years later.

1937: **Spanish Earth** USA

Producer	Contemporary Historians Inc. New York
Director	Joris Ivens
Script	Joris Ivens
Camera	John Ferno, Joris Ivens
Editor	Helen van Dongen
Commentary	Written and narrated by Ernest Hemingway
Music	Spanish folksongs, arranged by Virgil Thomson and Marc Blitzstein
Sound	Columbia Workshop, CBS, supervised by Irving Reis

Sound recorded by Western Electric at Film Art Studios, Inc.
52 mins. sound b/w 35mm.
Première, Hollywood, 19 July 1937.

'Ernest Hemingway, who wrote *Farewell to Arms*, and Joris Ivens have produced a picture which, without sensationalism, gives a vivid and forceful idea of the honour and misery of the war in Spain. They risked their lives taking some of the shots in the battle area.

'The main theme is the defence of Madrid and the patriotism of its defenders: running parallel with this is the work of the peasants striving to irrigate the dust-dry fields to provide fertile crops for the soldiery.

'Shots in Madrid show the damage already done to that city, and also the dangers to the citizens who still remain in their homes. Pitiful processions of refugees show the conflict in all its grim reality, while a battle for a bridgehead demonstrates the unspectacular but deadly prosecution of modern warfare.

'Wisely enough, "horrors" such as mutilated bodies have been avoided, but to the imaginative they are present all the time, and the grim undercurrent of death's harvest is made all the more forcible by the

director's restraint. The picture is well put together and Ernest Hemingway's commentary, free from wordiness, is spoken with a sincerity which
matches the lesson the war scenes bring'. (*Film Weekly*, 11 November 1937)

Spanish Earth is Ivens' first war film. Its history shows the limits of
documentary film-making within commercial distribution. Although the
intention was to make a film which could play in cinemas – hence a certain
emphasis on 'big names' (Orson Welles, at the height of his radio career,
initially recorded the commentary, but was later replaced by Hemingway)
and endorsements by Eleanor Roosevelt amongst others – it failed to find
commercial distribution and remained within the confines of film societies.
A second intention – to give evidence of German and Italian intervention on
Franco's side against the Government – was partially achieved when the
film was shown at the League of Nations in Geneva, but as far as influencing
the policies of governments went, this aspect was ignored or neutralised.
Indeed the British censors cut all references to this aspect of the war before
allowing the film to be shown.
   A critical difficulty which the film ran into was the appeal to objectivity.
According to one – no doubt apocryphal – story, Ernst Lubitsch asked
Ivens after a showing why he hadn't shown the other side. Ivens'
explanation was that if he had crossed the lines and been found filming he
would probably have been shot.

Although others of Ivens' war films – like *Seventeenth Parallel* and *Le peuple et ses fusils* – take the inhabitants of a village and their collective work and organisation as a central organising point, *Spanish Earth* is the only one to use an individual to link fighting front and home front. This continuity line survived from an original outline, but by no means constitutes the meat of the film. Its importance for the editing has been indicated by Helen van Dongen:

'The camera crew went to Spain while I stayed behind in New York . . . We had planned to follow the adventures of one Loyalist soldier behind the lines and in combat. After several sequences had been filmed, the boy was killed in action . . . Hemingway and Ivens constructed story-line after story-line to give shape and meaning to their daily experiences in Spain. All had point, some were filmed, but none stood forth and challenged attention as the central theme they were looking for . . .

'Sooner or later you realise that you cannot force your material, that you must give yourself up to it, let it work on your imagination, and that the ideas and feelings which this method produces are more trustworthy than any preconceived plans. In the case of *Spanish Earth* I had a deadline to meet, but I knew I could not hurry the editing. So I screened the material over and over, hoping for ideas to come, and in the meantime I divided it into categories according to subject. All the scenes of the bombings of Madrid, Valencia and Barcelona I linked together, and did the same with scenes of front-line combat, life behind the lines, and so on. And in the midst of all this screening and categorizing, something began to happen. In one sequence the soldier Julian returns home on furlough and is greeted by his mother and sister in the village street. Where was his father, I wondered? Then I remembered that in quite a different collection of scenes, those dealing with farming, there was a shot in which a boy ran out into the fields and said something to a farmer, who dropped his hoe and ran back towards the village. Of course! This was the father, being told of his son's return; these scenes belonged together as part of the same pattern. In joining the two scenes, I not only built my homecoming sequence to its completion, but had found the link I was looking for between the labourers in the field and the soldiers whom their labour fed.' (Richard Griffith, 'Helen van Dongen', in *New Movies*. Nov-Dec 1943, pp.27–8)

Soon after the release of *The Spanish Earth* a new production company was formed, comprising some of the same group of writers who were involved in *The Spanish Earth*, to sponsor a film on China. Money was raised in Hollywood and, with the help of Luise Rainer, star of *The Good Earth* (Sidney Franklin, 1937, based on the Pearl Buck novel), from the Chinese community in New York. Ivens was again to be the director, John Ferno the cameraman, and they were joined in China by the Hungarian war photographer Robert Capa, whose work was also to be financed by *Life* magazine.

Japan had begun its incursions into Manchuria in September 1931, and had set up a puppet state of Manchukuo in 1932. The Kuomintang, led by Chiang Kai-shek, at first followed a policy of negotiating with the Japanese, agreeing to the neutralisation of North China and the suppression of anti-Japanese agitation there. Chiang Kai-shek's over-riding concern was the elimination of the Communist Party, whose forces established a new base, in the North-West at Yenan in 1935. However, his northern allies, Manchurian warlords, were discontented with a strategy which sent them to fight Chinese in North West China rather than Japanese, who were using their base to extend their area of control to the South and West. At the end of 1936 Chiang Kai-shek was kidnapped at Sian and forced to agree in principle to a united front with the communists against the Japanese. This united front was officially set up in September 1937, three months after Japanese forces had invaded Peking and open war had broken out. By the end of 1937 the Japanese had captured the main coastal area as far south as Shanghai and considerable territory inland, including the Kuomintang capital, Nanking. A base was then established in Hankow, whilst the Japanese advance continued. It was during the Hankow period that Ivens, Ferno and Capa arrived in China. They witnessed and filmed part of the battle of Taierchwang, near Soochow in Shantung province, the only major set-back in the Japanese advance to Chengchow. By the end of 1938 Hankow itself had been captured, the Kuomintang base moving west once more to Chungking in Szechuan province.

Ivens, Ferno and Capa were thus working in a situation of defeat for the Kuomintang forces to which they were attached and of severe internal political strain. Any alternative representative of Chinese nationalism – for example, Mme Sun Yat-sen – had to be filmed without the knowledge of the Kuomintang, and it was a decisive, if confused, moment of Chinese politics. Their work was hampered by the interference of Kuomintang censors, who attempted to control all filming and feared that too much prominence might be given to their communist allies if the crew were allowed access to the North-West and the Eighth Route Army. Nonetheless, Ivens did make contact with the communists, arranging to leave them a camera and some reels of film for use in the Yenan base. It was this camera which has been exhibited in the Museum of the Revolution in Peking.

1938: **The Four Hundred Million** USA

Producer	History Today Inc.
Director	Joris Ivens
Script	Joris Ivens
Camera	John Ferno, Robert Capa
Editor	Helen van Dongen
Music	Hanns Eisler
Commentary	Dudley Nichols, spoken by Fredric March

53 mins. sound b/w 35mm.
Première: 7 March 1939, New York.

'In *400 Million* several sequences were cut to my music – bombardment, dust-storm; the music composed for the children sequence was cut and edited to fit the picture . . . The battle scene of *400 Million* would lead an inexperienced composer to write typical battle music . . . But an analysis of the sequence, with the help of some vivid details (artillery placed under blossoming trees, wounded soldiers, refugees, the armoured train, etc.) suggest a music which must express the contradiction in this sequence, very important for the audience's understanding. Even in a fight for a good cause . . . music needn't be reduced to flag-waving. So my music expressed the energy and the strain . . . After a careful analysis of picture details, a musical form was suggested which gave me the opportunity to change the character of the music without interrupting its flow and logic: the themes and variation form.' (Hanns Eisler, in *Films* No. 4 1940, pp.8–10)

The footage shot by Ivens' crew was supplemented by newsreel material, particularly that shot by H S Wong in Shanghai. Chinese dialogue was post-synched by New York Chinese. Some of the footage of the battle of Taierchwang was used in a film called *China Fights*, a fiction film featuring a heroic Kuomintang officer, which is sometimes wrongly attributed to Ivens. Like *Spanish Earth*, *400 Million* failed to find the commercial distribution it was aimed for, and its most receptive audience turned out to be those already involved – the Chinese population in America in this case. The film was banned in England and France. When it was finally released in London, in November 1939, all references to fascism had been cut.

4   Sojourn in the USA: 1938–45

Ivens' next film was to be made in America, the America of the mid-West. He was approached with a project by Pare Lorentz, the American documentarist whose first films – *The Plow that Broke the Plains* (1936) and *The River* (1937) – had been successful enough to hold out the promise that documentary might become box office. Lorentz became head of the United States Film Service, a department set up by the Roosevelt Administration as a form of government film sponsorship, which was broken by congressional opposition. The commissioning body for Ivens' film, *Power and the Land*, was the Department of Agriculture. Their objective was to demonstrate the benefits of rural electrification for the small farmer. For the purposes of the film, Ivens' team, which included Floyd Crosby, a cameraman who also worked with Flaherty, concentrated on the life of one family – the Parkinsons. In the course of this work, Ivens was able to deepen his experience of working with non-actors and, hand in hand with this, of the technique of re-enactment.

1939–40: **Power and the Land** USA
Producer   US Film Service, Washington DC, in collaboration
                                        with the US Dept. of Agriculture

Director	Joris Ivens
Script	Edwin Locke, Joris Ivens
Camera	Floyd Crosby, Arthur Ornitz
Editor	Helen van Dongen
Music	Douglas Moore
Commentary	Stephen Vincent Benet, spoken by
	William P Adams

Made with the participation of the Parkinson family and the members of the Belmon Electric Cooperative, St Clairsville, Ohio.
33 mins. sound b/w 35mm.
Première: October 1941, St Clairsville, Ohio.

'The original script showed a day's work on the farm without electricity. The Department of Agriculture wanted this as an historical record of the work of the farmer before the Rural Electrification Administration brought electricity. This made us see the film as a simple before-and-after story; done with enough colour and delicacy, it would work out. When I realised that I could not include the drama of the conflict between farmers and private utilities, this before-and-after story was the best alternative. Getting the electricity would be a kind of simple transition. We indicated somewhere in the commentary that before the coming of electricity there were fights.

'The documentary film has always one great force, individual styles notwithstanding – that is, that it is taken on the spot. This gives an authenticity it must always have – too much emphasis on re-enactment can be hazardous. Sixty percent of a normal documentary film has nothing to do with acting . . . There will always be certain themes which will be best carried out in a purely documentary style. There are others that demand considerable re-enactment, and by re-enactment I mean the reconstruction of an emotional situation, not merely recreating a familiar act . . .

'Our farm film presented material that seemed to demand re-enactment. The ease with which the subject took shape as soon as we decided on this re-enactment treatment seemed to prove that we were right . . .

'Working for months with the same persons, you can gradually expect to find more acceptance of themselves as actors. The non-actors become more flexible and adaptable, and greater demands can be made on them, they can be taught something of the film's technique.

'When Bill Parkinson couldn't understand why he had to repeat an action more than once whilst the camera was shifted about for a total shot, medium, or close-up, I took him to see a movie at the local theatre at St Clairsville, a gangster film with James Cagney. I pointed out how an action in a finished film was made out of long shots, medium shots and close-ups. From then on he understood our editing and continuity problems and gave very useful assistance . . .

'I used another technique to work with Bip, Bill's eight-year old son. Early in the morning I went alone with Bip to the corn field where we were

to shoot an action with his father and a sunflower in the afternoon. As a kind of secret between us, Bip and I acted out the scene which would later be filmed with his father. All the directions were given with nobody around. For the actual shooting in the afternoon I didn't need to tell him what to do, or how to do it – he felt relaxed and sure of himself. Had I given the directions with the others around "now you have to go to the right, pick up the flower" and so forth, he would have resisted completely or acted badly.'
(Joris Ivens, *The Camera and I*, pp.190–193)

Power and the Land was used for many years as an informational film by the Department of Agriculture, and in this way reached a very wide audience.

With Floyd Crosby as cameraman Ivens then began work on another film, provisionally entitled *New Frontiers*. However this project came to a halt because of disagreements between Ivens and his producers, the Sloan Foundation and the New York University Educational Film Institute. The unedited footage has been lost.

His next appointment, in 1941, was as a teacher at the University of Southern California, where he lectured on the principles of documentary film-making. It was also during 1941 that, encouraged by Jay Leyda, he began work on his autobiography, *The Camera and I*. During these years, however, the World War was spreading. In 1940 Germany had invaded Holland, which was reduced to the status of 'subject territory', and in 1941 its attack was turned against the Soviet Union. There was increasing pressure for the United States to become involved in the War, although it was not to do so until later, after the Japanese attack on Pearl Harbour. Ivens' next film, which he co-directed with Lewis Milestone, was a compilation film, *Our Russian Front*, made up of material shot by Russian cameramen, including Roman Karmen, and was designed as a plea for intervention and solidarity with the Russians.

1941: **Our Russian Front** USA

Producer	Art Kino, New York
Director of Production	Helen van Dongen
Directors	Joris Ivens, Lewis Milestone
Editor	Marcel Craven
Commentary	Elliot Paul, spoken by Walter Huston
Music Supervision	Dmitri Tiomkin
Music	Dmitri Shostakovitch, Hanns Eisler
Cameramen	Roman Karmen, Ivan Belakov, Arkadi Shafran and others

38 mins. sound b/w 35mm.

After this film was completed Ivens worked on a commercial venture to help clear his debts. He had no control over the editing or commentary, and does not count the film as one of his own:

1942: **Oil for Aladdin's Lamp** USA
Producer   J Walter Thompson, for Shell Oil
Director   Joris Ivens

Ivens was extremely keen to be involved in the war effort, and had suggested a series of film 'letters to the President' to be produced by the US Office of Information. Only one of these was made: 'A sailor on convoy duty to England'; but in Canada, not the United States, and by the National Film Board of Canada, which John Grierson had taken charge of in 1939 and whose activities he had expanded enormously.

1942–43: **Action Stations** Canada
Producer   National Film Board of Canada
Director   Joris Ivens
Script   Joris Ivens
Camera   Osmond Borrodaille, François Villiers
Editor   Joris Ivens
Commentary   Malcolm, spoken by Allen Field
50 mins. (approx.) sound b/w 35mm.
Première: Canada, 1943

Shot on board the corvette *Port Arthur*, on which Ivens lived for four months, the film shows the life of those who man an escort ship and the constant threat of submarine attack which they face.

After completing *Action Stations* Ivens returned to the United States. He made no more films of his own for the rest of the war, but participated in the following projects:

1943: With Carl Foreman as script-writer and Helen van Dongen as assistant, Ivens worked on the production of a three-hour compilation film, to be called *Know Your Enemy, Japan*. This film was to be part of the extremely eclectic *Why We Fight* series, produced by Frank Capra for the US War Department Special Service Division. Footage from *The Spanish Earth* and *The Four Hundred Million* was included in other films in this series, including Anatole Litvak's mediocre *China Fights*. *Know Your Enemy, Japan* ran into trouble after the US Government changed its policy towards the Japanese Emperor, and declared that he would not be treated as a war criminal. The line of the film was to show his connections with the power base of Japanese fascism. Ivens refused to accept this political change of direction, and stopped working on the film.

1944: With the French scriptwriter Vladimir Pozner, with whom he was later to work in the German Democratic Republic after the Second World War, Ivens worked on a scenario, *Woman of the Sea*, which was proposed to Greta Garbo. After consultations with the Swedish government, which was neutral in the war, she turned the script down.

1945: As technical adviser, Ivens worked on the documentary aspects of the script of William Wellman's *The Story of G.I. Joe.*

His cinematic life was beginning to move in another direction, though. In October 1944 the Dutch government in exile appointed Ivens Film Commissioner for the Dutch East Indies, with Helen van Dongen as Deputy Commissioner. The appointment was to begin immediately, although as long as the Japanese were in occupation not much more could be done than gather equipment. With Japanese defeat in 1945, Ivens set out for Indonesia, arriving first in Sydney, Australia, where he began to plan future film work with members of the Indonesian government in exile and a crew assembled from Canada (Don Fraser), the United States (Marion Michelle) and Australia (Catherine Duncan). It quickly became clear that the Dutch government was not going to grant independence to Indonesia, however, and on 21 November 1945, Ivens resigned his post, stating at a press conference that he could not reconcile the Government's promises of autonomy to Indonesia with their present attitude. Nor could he reconcile their present attitude with his contract which asked him to 'demonstrate the building of a future Indonesia in which Dutch and Indonesians can and must co-operate on the footing of complete equality and mutual respect.' His statement ended by declaring that 'there is a road to freedom for all peoples, and the documentary film should record and assist this progress'.

5 Left Politics and Cinema II: 1946–56

Ivens' conception of the role of the documentary and his own role as a film-maker entailed, in this situation, putting his resources at the service of the new Indonesian Government rather than at the service of the Dutch Government. From having been a stopping-off point, Australia became the location for his next film, a record of Australian support for the Indonesian republic. Political and technical conditions meant a return to the methods of *Borinage* – use of the Kinamo, semi-clandestinity, the attempt at an agitational film which could make a direct political intervention. This film, *Indonesia Calling*, when smuggled to Java became a weapon of the new government and in Australia served as a focus of post-war political activity. It is also said to be the first film shot in Australia which uses an Australian accent in its narration.

1946: **Indonesia Calling** Australia
Production   Waterfront Union of Australia, Sydney
Director   Joris Ivens
Script   Joris Ivens
Camera   Marion Michelle
Editor   Joris Ivens
Commentary   Catherine Duncan, spoken by Peter Finch
22 mins. sound b/w 35mm.
Première: September 1946, Sydney.

Marion Michelle: I had to shoot one part from high on a bridge, which was difficult to reach. To get a shot of the docks I had to lean over with the camera. And I suffered from vertigo. But no-one else could do it. The first cameraman immediately distanced himself from the film, the second realised that he wouldn't make very much money, the third just melted away.

Catherine Duncan: That was a really difficult problem: it was underground work, with inadequate equipment, no money, up against the police, and, given the urgency of the situation, you had to film whenever anything happened as well.

MM: A republic had just been proclaimed in Indonesia, but the Dutch refused to recognise its independence, notwithstanding the Atlantic Charter, and they started direct intervention. During the war the eighteen ships of the Dutch colonial navy, with their Indonesian crews, had been stationed in Australian ports. The Dutch wanted to use these ships in order to recapture their old colony. At that point the Indonesian crews went on strike and stopped the ships from leaving.

Whilst they had been in Australia the Indonesian seamen had formed their first trade union, and their strike was supported by the Australian seamens' and dockers' unions; as well as by Chinese, Indian, Dutch and British sailors. Because of this those eighteen ships were halted for two years – enough to give the young republic a breathing space.

CD: This of course meant that most of the shots had to be taken in the docks, which was a prohibited area immediately after the war. Since the principal actors were Indonesians, with dark skins, it was difficult to make them pass for Australians.

MM: And the shooting stock! It was impossible to buy brand-new film, and you could never gauge the sensitivity of waste stock . . . For the filming there was only an old Kinamo, which didn't work very well. It was a grotesque situation! When Ivens arrived in Australia he was received officially because he was a government functionary. For the first time in his life he could have the best possible equipment. But he had no time to use it because he resigned shortly afterwards. So instead he found himself in an extremely unofficial position, using his Kinamo, his first camera, which he had used to make *The Bridge*.

CD: His experience with *Borinage* came in useful at that point!

MM: Yes, he organised shooting like guerilla warfare. He would tell a particular group of Indonesians to arrive separately and in disguise, then to assemble at a precise point in order to carry out a specific action, and then to disperse as quickly as they could. All of this had to be prepared down to the last detail, so as not to attract attention. Anyway his advice was always followed scrupulously. I thought that these people were sure to win if this was the way they organised.

CD: But what happened with the filming that wasn't planned like that? As far as I remember, Joris told me that you wrote the script as soon as the film was finished.

MM: The script was written according to whatever happened each day. Sometimes we knew what was going to happen, but for the most part we found out at the last moment or by chance that something interesting was going to take place, usually at dusk. That meant that we always had to be ready to step in.

CD: At the end we had 25 minutes of material with which to make a 20 minute film. When we saw the raw material in Murph's cinema, he told me that if Ivens could make a film out of that stuff, then he – Murph – could make *Ben Hur* outside in the courtyard.

MM: But Murph had never seen Joris at work. It was a real miracle! As the work went on the shots took shape and became dramatic. Joris was a magician in the editing room.

CD: One thing is certain – the Australian audience saw themselves in that film. Watching the film they realised for the first time that they and their country had an important role to play in world affairs.

MM: I believe that the film was a passionate adventure for everyone – as much for those who saw it as for those who participated. Murph was never paid for the use of his cinema. Peter Finch, who spoke the commentary, never received a fee. Our 'actors' – the Chinese, Indian, Indonesian and Australian trades unionists or dockers – saw the film as an enrichment of their lives. It has a spontaneity, an enthusiasm, a freshness which bursts on to the screen, even now, whenever you see the film.

CD: And that night when we first showed their film to the Indonesians, packed like sardines and squatting on the floor in Murph's cinema, they were so near to the film that you couldn't tell where the public ended and the film began.

MM: Afterwards the film was shown in many different countries, but there is one showing I'm sorry to have missed!

CD: The first showing in Indonesia.

MM: There was a 16mm print with a Malay commentary which was sent on a small sailing ship via Singapore and was sneaked into Indonesia despite a Dutch blockade. This happened at a time when Dutch radio was broadcasting to the Indonesians that they were isolated, that no-one supported them and they should give up. Then the film arrived, demonstrating a history of solidarity and international aid. It was projected in the open air in public places and became an arm of the independence struggle.

CD: Perhaps it is that which makes working with Joris such a vital experience. One has the feeling that these films are important, that they are

43

part of world history. Everyone has the impression that they are personally responsible for the film. Joris is able to draw the best out of those who work with him. I can't remember him ever rejecting a suggestion or an idea.

MM: One has only to discuss an idea with him to see it transformed, thanks to some mysterious combination with other ideas, into an element which inevitably leads into the finished film. It might be valuable or not, but it had some use, one knew that immediately, and that was pleasing. Every step forward seemed to us the only, the inevitable solution.

CD: Yes, we always worked so closely together that it was difficult to delineate our respective roles. I wrote most of the commentary at the editing table, so that it developed along with the editing. For us no problem existed separately from others. We were composing a work in which sometimes the image, sometimes the commentary, sometimes the music or the sound effects were primary. I had power not only over the words, but over a whole orchestra of emotional and intellectual possibilities. But all the same I was subjected to a very strict discipline, like the discipline of composing a sonnet.

MM: As Joris says: 'The real film is created and reproduced in the cinema, between the screen and the audience'. (Catherine Duncan and Marion Michelle, in *Joris Ivens*, DDR, 1963)

One effect of *Indonesia Calling* was that Ivens' passport was taken from him by the Dutch Government. Until 1956, when his full citizenship rights were restored, he worked in Eastern Europe, taking up residence first of all in Prague in 1947.

It was on the initiative of Lubomir Linhart, director of the Czech State Film Organisation, that Ivens made his first film in the new People's Democracies, *The First Years*, which is dedicated to the task of post-war reconstruction. In its final version it comprises episodes shot in Bulgaria, Czechoslovakia and Poland. A Yugoslav episode was originally included, but a serious rift in relations between the Yugoslav and Soviet governments, which led to the expulsion of Yugoslavia from the Cominform and its exclusion from the 'anti-imperialist' camp, meant that this episode was not finally included. (Cominform was the international organisation of communist parties set up after the Second World War in response to pressure from the Yugoslav party. It was a short-lived organisation and its main operation was the co-ordination of an Eastern European and Soviet boycott of the Marshall Plan.)

1949: Pierwsze Lata (The First Years) Czechoslovakia; Bulgaria; Poland

Producers	Statni Film, Prague; Witwornia Filmow Documentalnych, Warsaw; Bulgar Film, Sofia
Executive Producer	Jaroslav Jilovec
Director	Joris Ivens
Script	Marion Michelle

Editors	Joris Ivens, Karel Hoeschl
Commentary	Catherine Duncan, spoken by Stanley Harrison
	(English version), Karel Hoeschl (Czech version)
Music	Jan Kapr, performed by the Czech Philharmonic
	Orchestra under the direction of Otakar Parik
Sound Engineer	Emil Polednik

Bulgarian Episode – Camera: Zachari Shandov, Ivan Fric; Asst. camera: Dmitri Kitanov; Production delegate: Nikolai Tankov
Czech Episode – Camera: Ivan Fric; Asst. camera: Josej Molhanek; Asst. director: Karel Kabelac; Production delegate: Miloslav Jilovec
Polish Episode – Camera: Wladislaw Forbert; Asst. camera: M Wiesolek; Production delegate: W Hollander.
99 mins. sound b/w 35mm.
Première: December 1949, Prague.

The Bulgarian Episode is shot in the village of Radilovo, where the main crop is tobacco and the conditions of drought make the occupants dependent on rain. Through regional planning and irrigation systems, this dependence will be ended. At the end of the film a child is born, and the final text reads: 'A child needs twenty years in order to become a man. But this one here will know what the future will bring him. He will not depend any longer on the benevolence of the rain.' This final text became the starting point for a Bulgarian television film, *Masters of the Rain*, made in colour in September 1968 in the same village, and shown at celebrations of Ivens' seventieth birthday in 1968 at the Leipzig Festival of Documentary Films. In an interview recorded in Paris in 1976, Ivens talked about the experience of making this section of the film:

'In 1947, shortly after the Second World War, I was in Bulgaria and made a film called *The First Years*. It was a question of showing the extremely difficult and complex task of effecting the transformation of a capitalist society into a socialist society. In Bulgaria, in a small village where peasants lived and cultivated tobacco, I filmed the birth of a child. Not the course of the confinement itself, but everything that happened before. Whilst the woman, lying on the bed, was awaiting the birth, a cow was turning constantly in the courtyard, and one saw a middle-aged woman boiling water and moving about restlessly . . . Thus I showed that the child was going to be born in a farm. This whole scene was concentrated in a symbolic manner. They were awaiting the rain, which would fertilise the earth, etc . . . In the end all this was very realist and filmed – you could almost touch reality with your fingertips. When the film was finished and shown, some Bulgarian Party officials who were in charge of art said: 'Yes, very good, but we have maternity hospitals in our villages'. I said: 'Perhaps, but I didn't see any in this province.' 'Yes, that is probably true, but you should show maternity hospitals – that would be socialist realism because it is the future, our future. Everything else, what you have filmed, has become a part of the past.' This was stupid, because it was not the past at all. 'You must film the future, that is the reality', they said. 'In this way, one would see neither the reality nor the future. That is in principle false.' (Interview with *Filmfaust*, 11/12 October 1976)

The Czech episode tells the story of Czech nationalism since Jan Huss, and reconstructs the link between Czech industry, symbolised in the major shoe firm, BATA, and German fascism. When Germany takes over in Czechoslovakia, Huss's statue is covered over with the Nazi flag, the swastika – a touch reminiscent of *Hangmen Also Die*. After the war, a new social and economic order is to be constructed. The film ends with Gottwald's speech outlining the first Five Year Plan.

The Polish episode, structured like a fiction film, follows the story of a music teacher who leaves devastated Warsaw, where her family has been killed, and travels west to the new areas of Silesia ceded to Poland by Germany after the end of the war. There she works in a steel factory as a laboratory assistant and, after an emergency in the factory, overcomes her initial alienation to become involved in the life of the factory and of its workers.

In 1950 Ivens moved to Poland, where he taught a course at the Lodz film school and married. The period 1947–49 was the moment of formation of the 'Cold War', the division of the world on new political grounds. It was no longer war-time alliances which mattered, but choices of political systems and economic agreements determined by splits between the erstwhile allies – in particular the USA and the USSR. Ivens' work thus inserted itself into a new political reality. Most of his films from this period involve international co-operation within a socialist network.

1951: **Pokoj Zwyciezy Swiat** (Peace will Win) Poland

Producer	Wytwornia Filmow Dokumentalnych, Warsaw
Directors	Joris Ivens, Jerzy Bossak
Script	Jerzy Bossak
Camera	Wladislaw Forbert, K Chodura, F Srednicki, F Fuchs, S Sprudin, K Szczecinski and others
Editor	Joanna Rojewska
Music	Jerzy Gert, Wladislaw Szpilman
Commentary	S Arski, F Malcuzinski, B Viernik. In America, Howard Fast. In France, Louis Daquin

90 mins. (approx.) sound b/w 35 mm.

In 1951 the World Peace Council planned to meet in Sheffield, but the Attlee Government in Britain refused entry to its delegates, including Pablo Picasso, who, on being turned away, vowed never to set foot in England again, and never did. The Congress then took place in Warsaw, and this is a record of its proceedings.

46

Jerzy Bossak, who co-directed and scripted the film, had been head of the documentary film studios in Warsaw until 1948, when he resigned and concentrated on production work. After 1956 he became a teacher at the Lodz Film School, and also worked as artistic director of the Warsaw documentary studios as well as being head of the production unit 'Kamera'.

Ivens' next film was a Russian-German co-production.

1952: **Freundschaft Sieft** (Friendship Triumphs) USSR; DDR

Production	Mosfilm, Moscow; DEFA-Documentarfilm, Berlin
Directors	Ivan Pyriev, Joris Ivens
Assistant Directors	A Frolov, D Vasiliev, A Thorndike
Script	Ivan Pyriev, A Frolov
Camera	V Pavlov, V Mikocha, J Manglovski and others
Editors	A Kulganek, K Moskvina
Music	Isaac Dunajevski
Lyric	M Matussovski
Commentary	S Antonov

95 mins. (approx.) sound colour 35mm.
Première: April 1952, Berlin.

Ivens' first colour film, *Freundschaft Siegt* is a film chronicle of the International Youth Conference held in Berlin in 1951. Twenty four cameramen were in the crew, twelve from the Soviet Union, twelve from the German Democratic Republic. This film won the Peace Prize at the Karlovy Vary Film Festival in 1952. Andrew Thorndike, an assistant on this film, made a major contribution to the growth of the East German cinema.

1952: **Wyscig Pokoju Warszawa-Berlin-Praga** (Friedensfahrt 1952; Peace Tour 1952) Poland; GDR

Producers	Wytwornia Filmow Dokumentalnych, Warsaw; DEFA-Documentarfilm, Berlin
Director	Joris Ivens
Script	Joris Ivens
Camera	Karel Szczecinski, Walter Feldmer, Jerzy Pyrkosz, Erich Barthel, Hans Dume, Ewald Krause
Editor	Krystyna Rutkowska
Music	Wernfried Hubel
Commentary	Eva Fiszer, spoken by Andrej Lapicki

Première: Warsaw 1952.
44 mins. sound colour 35mm.
A report on the annual amateur cycle race Warsaw-Berlin-Prague

Song of the Rivers, the last film which Ivens directed during this period, was commissioned by the communist-oriented World Federation of Trades Unions, based in Prague, an international organisation whose limits tended to be defined by the frontiers of the Cold War. This compilation film, which makes a classic use of montage, brought together material shot by cameramen in 32 different countries, and uses footage from *Borinage* and *New Earth* as well as a film on dockers made by Robert Menegoz, one of Ivens' assistants. 18 versions of the film were produced, and although *Song of the Rivers* was banned in many countries, it was seen by an estimated 250 million people – 40 million of them in China. The 'rivers' in the title refers to six major continental rivers – Mississippi, Ganges, Nile, Volga, Amazon and Yangtze – and to the seventh river, that of the working-class movement, meeting in Vienna.

1954: **Das Lied der Ströme** (Song of the Rivers) GDR

Producer	DEFA-Documentarfilm, Berlin in collaboration with the WRTU (World Federation of Trades Unions)
Executive Producer	Hans Wegner
Director	Joris Ivens
Assistant Directors	Joop Huisken, Robert Menegoz
Script	Vladimir Pozner, Joris Ivens
Camera	Erich Nitzschmann, Anatoli Koloschin, Sacha Vierny, Maximilian Scheer and others
Editor	Ella Ensink
Assistant Editor	Trante Vishnevsky

Commentary	Vladimir Poznere, spoken by Ernst Busch (German version) Claude Martin (French version) Alex McCrindle (English version)
Music	Dmitri Shostakovitch
Lyrics	Bertolt Brecht and Semion Kirsanov, sung by Paul Robeson and Ernst Busch
Sound Engineer	Heinz Reusch

90 mins. sound b/w 35mm.
Première: 17 September 1954, Berlin.

Song of the Rivers was shown at the Karlovy Vary Film Festival in 1954, where it received the prize dedicated to 'the struggle for a better life'. In 1954, too, it received the International Peace Prize awarded by the World Peace Council. The French critic Georges Sadoul was at the Karlovy Vary Festival and reported on the film in *Cahiers du Cinéma*:

'Summoned by this cinematographic Orpheus, the Nile and the Amazon, the Ganges and the Congo, the Volga and the Yangstze, unite their waters and the people who throng around them. This hymn to men's grandeur, to the struggle which transforms poverty into splendour, this proud, open song, brings a great director to the high point of his art. However, Ivens considers that the version presented in Karlovy Vary . . . is a sort of "work in progress". He is working on the French version, which will be shown in Paris by the end of the year. *Song of the Rivers* was one of the major discoveries of the festival . . .' (Georges Sadoul, *Cahiers du Cinéma*, No. 40, November 1954)

The French version was in fact banned for commercial distribution in France.

Ivens continued his collaboration with DEFA after *Song of the Rivers*, working as artistic advisor or supervisor on the following films:

1956: *Mein Kind* (My Child), directed by Vladimir Pozner and Alfons Machalz. Critics' Prize, Mannheim, 1956.

1956: With Alberto Cavalcanti as co-supervisor, *Die Windrose* (The Windrose), an episode film shot in five countries: Brazil (Director, Alex Viany); USSR (Director, Sergei Gerassimov); France (Director Yannik Bellon); Italy (Director, Gillo Pontecorvo); China (Director, Wu Kuo-yin)

1956: Ivens acted as adviser to Gérard Philipe, on the French/German co-production *Les aventures de Till L'Espiegle* (The adventures of Till Eulenspiegel).

When, in 1956, the Dutch Government returned Ivens' passport, he decided to return to Western Europe, taking up residence in Paris, where he still lives.

6 The Flying Dutchman: 1957–66

La Seine a rencontré Paris was Ivens' first film in what was to be a crowded period of films and travel. It was also the first film made by a new production company, Garance Films, set up by Betsy Blair, Roger Pigaut and Serge Reggiani.

1957: **La Seine a rencontré Paris** France

Producer	Garance-Film, Paris
Director	Joris Ivens
Assistant Director	Guy Blanc
Script	Joris Ivens, from an idea by Georges Sadoul
Camera:	André Demaître, Philipe Brun
Editor:	Gisèle Chézeau
Commentary:	Poem written by Jacques Prévert, spoken by Serge Reggiani
Music:	Philippe Gérard

32 mins. sound b/w 35mm.
Première: Paris, 20 November 1957
Prizes: Best Documentary, Cannes Festival, 1958; Best Documentary, San Francisco Festival, 1958; Oberhausen Festival, 1959

'The brief sequence with mannequins on the embankment was "organised documentary". I had observed this scene when acting as a kind of "film scout" some months earlier. Should we have deprived ourselves of it? A fundamental idea of the film was to show Parisians strolling, loving, working beside the Seine, to give a portrait of their life through the river. In order to represent Paris as the capital of high fashion and to show the aristocratisation of its banks which begins at Pont Sully, Ivens needed the mannequins and their photographer. Should he have adopted an extreme conception of *"cinéma vérité"* and waited for several months for a miraculous opportunity to allow him to find it unexpectedly? Of course not. Especially since it is a mannequin's *métier* to pose. Their behaviour would in no way be modified by the presence of another camera one morning next to their photographer. And when Ivens had recourse to a piece of documentary *mise en scène*, placing a fisherman with a dead fish on his line beside the Seine and having him pull it out at the moment of filming, he was not wrong at all. In this way he mixed the richness of popular life and the extraordinariness of a permanent spectacle on the Seine. . .

'What is more debatable is the idea (for which I am responsible) of including two lawyers, seen getting out of their car in their black robes and running away. This is a typical "bad good idea". First and foremost because I had never seen such a scene, but had thought up all the different parts of the gag, which Joris' assistants benevolently acted out, dressing up in lawyers' robes. You have to be a real Parisian to realise that the cars were parked by the Pont Neuf, just two steps from the law courts, and if you weren't French you would not know that our lawyers wear black robes with white bands. We were amused by the idea, but it remained a "private joke".

'I don't think that there are any others in the film. "Organised documentary" was reduced to a minimum. It stands to reason that it would have been shocking, even immoral, to have reconstructed one of the most moving moments of the film: a poor man, unemployed or a tramp, is sitting on a bench. Near him children are playing, dancing and singing, but he is alone. He has his lunch. He drinks wine, eats a little bread, and with pitiful sadness throws some crumbs to the birds. To have staged this would have meant falling into 1880s genre painting or melodramatic tear-jerker. [. . .]

'This scene was the fruit of much patience, but this doesn't prevent some from talking about reconstruction, and claiming that the man with the birds looks complicitly at the camera. . . You have to know the cinema, and Ivens' work, very badly to be able to fall into this fantastic interpretation. And if he could have made this film with the equipment which became available after 1960 it is certain that he would have recorded noises and sounds at the same time as the images, thanks to a synchronised recording system. If this proof to the ear had been added to the proof by the eye, no one would have dreamed of contesting this little piece of *"cinéma vérité"*. (Georges Sadoul, Introduction to A. Zalzman, *Joris Ivens*, Seghers, Paris 1963)

Then, in 1958, Ivens was invited to teach a film course in China at the Academy of Cinema, the first of many such appointments which combined education and film-making. 1958 was the year of the Great Leap Forward, of an increasing emphasis on Chinese self-reliance. *Before Spring*, the film he made there, was partly designed to help test colour film stock in a variety of climatic conditions. Whilst in China, Ivens witnessed the first withdrawal of Soviet experts and aid, an early symptom of what was to become a major split, and a significant political experience for him.

1958: **Before Spring** (French title, Lettres de Chine) China

Producer:	Central Studios for Newsreel and Documentary, Peking
Director:	Joris Ivens
Script:	Joris Ivens
Camera:	Wang Teh-tsieng, Shih Yi-min, Tsiao Tse-lin
Editor:	Joris Ivens
Commentary:	Ho Chung-hsin, spoken by Hsieh Tien
Music:	Kao Hu

38 mins. colour 35mm.
Première: Peking, 1958

'This practical work by cameramen from the Chinese Film School, which Ivens directed and signed at the end of the course of lectures he gave, is an attractive and lively film, and we can only regret that a too descriptive commentary is sometimes able to destroy the beauty of the images. A greater rigour in the script and a more poetic and less didactic commentary would perhaps have produced better results.

'Life in the harsh winter of Inner Mongolia constitutes the first part of the trilogy. Landscapes of snow and ice mingle with the slow pace of the camels and sheep. In the immensity of this country, man is present. As in most of Ivens' films he appears at work, taming a still wild nature. A few shots suffice for Ivens to show us how primitive the work is, what an arid desert the land.

'Man is even more present in the second part, *Spring Awakening*, where, with a laconic phrase and images of the construction of a reservoir, the face of modern China counterpoints its traditional one: "In China, 100 million people struggle each day to secure a water supply." They are engaged in gigantic work where every parcel of land must be utilised in order to feed six hundred million inhabitants: "This year they are putting the hills to wheat. Sterile ground will produce grain. They plan new cultivation." China is an immense construction site, where "monotony and solitude give place to life" and a call is made to future happiness.

'And then there is the Spring Festival (the Chinese New Year): snow and ice are left behind for fresh air, mulberries, fish, the symbols of abundance and good luck, children and their games. The Spring Festival is the occasion of a performance given by peasant actors: the representation of a centuries old legend, which always makes its audience laugh and cry. They cannot leave the village festivities without participating in the famous dragon dance which expresses joy at renewal.

'*Lettres de Chine*, with its decorative aspects, through which the traveller Ivens shows us elements far removed from Marco Polo, leaves us with the image of a people and a country which are alive and in the process of transformation'. (Robert Grelier, *Joris Ivens*, Paris 1965, pp. 102–3)

Whilst in Peking Ivens also made a short documentary on the demonstrations against the British landings in the Lebanon in 1958. It provides an early glimpse of the sort of Chinese demonstration which became more well-known during the Cultural Revolution.

1958: **600 Million With You** China

Producer:	Central Newsreel and Documentary Studios, Peking
Director:	Joris Ivens
Camera:	Cameramen from the Central Studio
Editor:	Joris Ivens

12 mins. sound b/w 35mm.
Première: Peking, 1958

On his return to Europe, Ivens was approached by Enrico Mattei, head of ENI, the Italian State Natural Gas Monopoly. Mattei, who died mysteriously in an air crash in 1962, and was the subject of a later film by Francesco

52

Rosi (*Il caso Mattei*, The Mattei Affair, 1972), had been put in charge of ENI on the understanding that he would wind it up. However, he expanded its activities and investment programme against much internal political opposition and external opposition from the US-controlled multinational oil firms. Ivens' films, collectively entitled *Italia non è un paese povero*, were to be shown on television. The first part, *Fuochi della Val Padana* (Fire in the Po Valley), deals with the extraction and distribution of methane in the Po Valley. The second part is divided in two: *Due città* (Two Cities), devoted to Venice (Porto Maghera) and Ravenna, is a treatment of the production of agipgaz and its by-products; and *La storia di due alberi* (*The Story of Two Trees*), set in Lucania, which contrasts the impoverishment of peasant life in a southern village, where seven families are dependent on one olive tree, with the future benefits to come through the newly exploited natural resource (mechanisms for controlling the gas outlets, lit up at night, are called 'Christmas trees').

The third part, *Appuntamento a Gela* (An Appointment in Gela), is set in Sicily, and revolves around the marriage of a Sicilian, daughter of a fisherman, to a North Italian worker on an oil rig offshore. By the time the film was finished, Mattei was in a weak political position, and RAI-TV refused to show the films as they were, taking particular exception to the representation of peasant life in Lucania as being irrelevant to the main subject. From being three programmes each 45 minutes long, the film was cut down and was shown, at Ivens' insistence, under the general description 'Fragments of a film by Joris Ivens'. He left the country secretly taking a complete copy with him, and this original version had its first showing at an Ivens retrospective in Modena in 1979.

Many of the younger generation of Italian directors worked with Ivens on the making of *Italia non è un paese povero*, including the Taviani brothers (Paolo and Vittorio, whose main success in England has been *Padre Padrone*, 1977), Valentino Orsini and Tinto Brass. A feature of the film is the consistent fun which is poked at TV documentary methods, in particular the technique of on-the-spot interviews.

1959: **L'Italia non è un paese povero** (Italy is not a Poor Country) Italy

Producer:	Proa Associated, Rome, in collaboration with ENI
Director:	Joris Ivens
Assistant Director:	Giovanni 'Tinto' Brass
Script:	Joris Ivens, Valentino Orsini, Paolo and Vittorio Taviani
Camera:	Mario Dolci, Oberdan Troiani, Mario Volpi
Editors:	Joris Ivens, Maria Rosada
Music:	Gino Marinuzzi
Commentary:	Alberto Moravia and Corrado Sofia, spoken by Enrico M Salerno

135 mins. (original version) sound b/w 35mm; cut by RAI-TV to 110 mins.

Mali was the next country in Joris Ivens' filmic itinerary. *Demain à Nanguila*, the only film made by Ivens in Africa, was one of the first films produced by the new Republic of Mali.

1960: **Demain à Nanguila** (Nanguila Tomorrow) Mali
Producer: Société Franco-Africaine de Cinéma
Director: Joris Ivens
Script: Catherine Varlin
Camera: Louis Miaille, Pierre Geuguen
Editors: Gisèle Chéseau, Hélène Arnal, Suzanne Baron
Music: Louis Bessière
Cast: Sidibe Moussa and the inhabitants of
                             Baukouman and Nanguila
50 mins. sound colour 35mm.
Première: Paris, 1960

The story of a young man, Sidibe Moussa, who becomes involved in the work of irrigation in his local community, and thus participates in the task of post-colonial construction in Africa.

After Mali, Cuba. ICAIC, the Cuban Institute of Cinema Art and centre of its national industry, invited Ivens to give a course of lectures and to make a film with his pupils. This was in the first years of the Castro government – Batista had been overthrown just two years before. *Pueblo armado* demonstrates the continuing threat of US-inspired and trained invasions with which the Cuban government lived. *Carnet de viaje* is much more impressionistic, a mixture of things seen, filmed and heard. This film was dedicated to Charlie Chaplin, after whom the first cinema club established after the revolution was named. A copy was sent to Chaplin in Switzerland.

1961: **Carnet de viaje** (Travel Notebook) Cuba
Production: ICAIC, Havana
Executive Producer: Saul Yelin (Cuba) Roger Pigaut (France)
Director: Joris Ivens
Assistant Directors: Jorge Fraga, Jose Massip (Cuba), Isabelle
                             Elizando, Guy Blanc (France)
Script: Joris Ivens
Camera: Ramon S Suarez, Jorge Herrera, Roberto
                             Larrabure, Gustave Maynolet
Editor: Hélène Arnal
Music: Harold Gramatgès
Commentary: Henri Fabiani, spoken by the author
Poem: Nicolas Guillen, spoken by the author
34 mins. sound b/w 35mm.
Première: Paris, 1961

1961: **Pueblo armado** (An Armed People) Cuba
Producer: ICAIC, Havana

Executive Producers:	Saul Yelin (Cuba), Roger Pigaut (France)
Director:	Joris Ivens
Script:	Joris Ivens
Camera:	Jorge Herrera, Ramon F Suarez
Editor:	Hélène Arnal
Music:	Harold Gramatgès
Commentary:	Henri Fabiani, spoken by Serge Reggiani

35 mins. sound b/w 35mm.
Première: Paris, 1961
This film was banned for commercial distribution in France.

'Fidel told me that they should profit from my being there by making a film about the people's militia; I accepted because I have always aimed through documentary to follow great historical events. . . A small group of counter-revolutionaries had just landed in Eastern Cuba. Their capture takes up the main part of the film.

'When Chris Marker arrived, he filmed the end of the period of mobilisation, the end of the alert, whereas I was there right at its highest pitch. I showed a people arming themselves to ward off a counter-attack. Chris, on the contrary, showed its disarmament. In fact one film completes the other, since the state of alert was terrible for them. I hope that they will never again be forced to take arms.' (Joris Ivens, interview with Raymond Bellour and Jean Michaut, *Cinéma 61*, No 56, May 1961)

The Marker film referred to here is *Cuba Sí!* (1961).

In 1962 Ivens was invited to Chile, to the Experimental Cinema Institute of the University of Santiago, to combine film-making and teaching once more. Together with students from the Institute he made two films. Before he left for Chile, work was completed on a film about the painter Chagall (*Marc Chagall, 1962*). Directed by Henri Langlois for the Cinémathèque Française, this film was four years in production (1958–62) and Ivens acted as editor throughout.

1962: **. . . A Valparaiso** Chile-France
Producers:	Argos-Films, Paris; Cine Experimental de la Universidad de Chile, Santiago
Director:	Joris Ivens
Script:	Joris Ivens
Assistants:	Sergio Bravo, Augustin Altez, Rebecca Yanez, Joaquin Olalla, Carlos Böker
Camera:	Georges Strouvé
Camera Assistants:	Patricio Guzman, Leonardo Martinez
Editor:	Jean Ravel
Music:	Gustavo Becerra, orchestra conducted by Georges Delerue
Song:	'Nous irons à Valparaiso', sung by Germaine Montero

Commentary: Chris Marker, spoken by Roger Pigaut
37 mins. b/w and colour 35mm.
Première: Paris, June 1963
Fipresci Prize, Oberhausen Festival, 1964.

Valparaiso as a city was much loved by the Chilean poet Pablo Neruda, who wrote about it in his memoirs in terms which evoke Ivens' film:

'The stairs start out from the bottom and from the top, winding as they climb. They taper off like strands of hair, give you a slight respite and then go straight up. They become dizzy. Plunge down. Drag out. Turn back. They never end.

'How many stairs? How many steps to the stairs? How many feet on the steps? How many centuries of footsteps, of going down and back with a book, tomatoes, fish, bottles, bread? How many thousands of hours have worn away the steps, making then into little drains where the rain runs down playing and crying?

'Stairways!

'No other city has spilled them, shed them like petals into its history, down its own face, fanned them into the air and put them together again as Valparaiso has. No city has had on its face these furrows where lives come and go, as if they were always going up to heaven or down into the earth. . .

'If we walk up and down all of Valparaiso's stairs we will have made a trip around the world.' (Pablo Neruda, *Memoirs*, Souvenir Press, London 1977, p. 61)

Chris Marker, whose commentary makes a great contribution to the film, was not on location in Valparaiso, but constructed the commentary in Paris on the basis of notes taken by Ivens during the filming. *A Valparaiso* is one of Ivens' most stunning films. The French critic, Robert Grelier, has noted that: '*Valparaiso* is one of the films in which Ivens is most rigorous in his scientific method. This rigour consists in establishing an analysis in a time which does not isolate the present, but links it to what happened before and after. It is a dialectical film which shows that history does not go by without leaving its imprint on men and on nature. In fact this city's past could not in any way be a refuge, a means of escaping present-day reality, as some tend to try to make us believe. And perhaps it is not by chance that having reached this conclusion, Ivens lets his eyes wander over a wall where "Cuba" has been written in a hasty scrawl. This word has a new ring to it, whose meaning is bound up with current perspectives of the future of Latin America.' (Grelier, p. 113) With footage of the circus at Valparaiso another film was made and a poem set to it by Jacques Prévert.

1963: **Le petit chapiteau** Chile-France
Producers: Argos-Film Paris; Cine Experimental de la
                              Universitad de Chile, Santiago, Chile

Director:	Joris Ivens
Camera:	Patricio Guzman
Editor:	Jean Ravel
Commentary:	Poem written and spoken by Jacques Prévert

6 mins. sound b/w 35mm.
Première: Paris, June 1963

Ivens' third film in Chile, and his first 16mm film, was a report on the election campaign of Salvador Allende, later President of Chile, who was killed in the right-wing coup of 1973.

1964: **Le train de la victoire** Chile

Producer:	FRAP (Fronte de Accion Popular)
Director:	Joris Ivens
Camera:	Patricio Guzman
Editor:	Sergio Bravo
Music:	Gustavo Becerra

9 mins. sound b/w 16mm.
with Salvador Allende

This film was originally commissioned by RTF the French Broadcasting Corporation, during a visit he made to France after filming *A Valparaiso*. At the last moment RTF cancelled the contract.

In 1963, from November 16 to 24, to celebrate Ivens' 65th birthday and 35th year of film-making, a major retrospective of his work was held in Leipzig, running in parallel with the Leipzig Documentary Festival. The following year a retrospective was held at the Filmmuseum in Amsterdam and Ivens was enthusiastically received back in his home country.

At the Mannheim Festival of 1964, Ivens figured near the top of the list of best documentary film-makers of all time. This list, arrived at by votes cast by 81 film critics and film historians from 12 countries, is interesting enough to bear reprinting: first Robert Flaherty, second Joris Ivens, then John Grierson, Basil Wright, Dziga Vertov, Sergei Eisenstein, Harry Watt, Walter Ruttmann, Luis Buñuel, Alain Resnais, Georges Rouquier, Pare Lorentz. The 12 best documentaries of all time, according to their votes, were *Nanook of the North, Night Mail, Turksib, Berlin, The Man with a Movie Camera, Louisiana Story, Farrébique, Nuit et brouillard, The General Line, Drifters, The Spanish Earth* and *Land Without Bread*.

Although such celebrations of Ivens' art might have been taken as the sign of a career nearing its end, projects and travel continued unabated. *Pour le Mistral* was to be his next film, set in the South of France, and doing for a wind what Ivens had once done for rain – making it cinematically visible and tangible. Few film-makers have treated the wind as a subject – Sjöström and Ivens are notable exceptions. Perhaps understandably *Pour le Mistral* was a difficult film to finance and plan, and although filming started in 1964, it had to be broken off and re-started in the spring of 1965.

1965: **Pour le Mistral** France

Producer:	Centre Européen Radio-Cinéma-Télévision
Director:	Joris Ivens
Assistant Directors:	Jean Michaud, Ariane Litaize, Michelle de Possel, Maurice Friedland, Bjorn Johanssen
Script:	Joris Ivens, René Guyonnet
Camera:	André Demaître, Pierre Lhomme, Gilbert Duhalde
Editors:	Jean Ravel, Emmanuele Castro
Music:	Luc Ferrari
Commentary:	André Verdet, spoken by Roger Pigaut

30 mins sound b/w and colour 35mm in CinemaScope
Première: Venice Film Festival, 1966

'I had been thinking about it for about five or six years before I finally decided to make the film. . . My first impulse towards it was given to me by the mistral itself, at St Tropez. The real mistral doesn't blow there, however – it's the place where it dies away. You can feel the struggle between two winds there – the mistral and the tramontane. It is a battle-line. Afterwards I met some people, including a wine-producer. I talked to them as we walked around and I realised that the wind was important for these people; it was concrete, it was real. I felt then that the wind was an excellent theme for a documentary. Perhaps because it perpetually moves, because it changes the colour of places, the atmosphere, people's psychology. . . All Provence is dominated by it. Its architecture, its history, its culture are all impregnated with it. Everyone has their own story to tell about it as well, usually more or less true.

'So I looked for a producer. This was difficult because it is a difficult subject, a capricious character who comes and blows as it likes, blows too hard or not at all, blows for a time and then goes away. . . Sometimes, when it doesn't come, you get the feeling that it is hiding, that it knows you want to film it. So nobody had much enthusiasm for this particular film-star. Not even the Centre du Cinéma, which didn't believe you could make a film about it. I had, however, written a treatment. . . A young, enthusiastic producer, Claude Nedjar, gave me the go-ahead to research the literature which dealt with the mistral – Hugo, Daudet, Giono and others had written about it; painters had spread it on their canvasses. My compatriot, Van Gogh, in particular, had produced eighty per cent of his paintings using the light of the mistral. I also had to study the history of meteorology since Greek and Roman times. Starting from all this and the relations between the wind and man, I wrote a screenplay in collaboration with René Guyonnet and Armand Gatti. For sound and music I used the research centre of the RTF. There were enormous problems because the wind is the deadly enemy of sound engineers: they avoid it, or always use the same recording of it. . .

'For my part I wanted different sounds and a young composer, Luc Ferrari, had the idea of creating special boxes to trap the sound of the wind.

And we went to try them out in Haute Provence in October 1963. In our film we show the relation of the wind to men and vice-versa. Some men, for example, fear the wind. Architects work to protect them from it. And see the part the wind plays in everyday life! But the wind has its friends as well: gliders, for example. And it doesn't just affect men, it affects animals too. . .'
(Joris Ivens, interviewed in *Cinéma 64*, June 1964.)

When *Pour le Mistral* was completed Ivens went for the first time to Vietnam. The Vietnamese war was to have some of the meaning for the sixties that the Spanish Civil War had for the thirties. US intervention in Vietnam had started in a big way in 1961, a year after the formation of the National Liberation Front in the South and two years after the opening of a communication and transport route, the 'Ho Chi Minh trail', from North to South. In 1965, the year Ivens visited Vietnam, the US had started a bombing campaign against the North, and this is a major theme of Ivens' film *Le ciel, la terre* (literally, The Sky, The Earth: English title 'The Threatening Sky'). With the bombing campaign, an international movement against the war grew, although the early sixties had produced student protest on a smaller scale and 'teach-ins'.

1965: **Le ciel, la terre** (The Threatening Sky) Vietnam; France

Producer:	Dovidis, Paris
Director:	Joris Ivens
Assistant Director:	Cao-Thuy
Camera:	Duc Hoa, Robert Destangue, Thoc Van
Editors:	Catherine Dourgnon, Françoise Beloux
Music:	Vietnamese folk music performed by L'Ensemble Artistique des Etudiants Vietnamiens en Paris.
Commentary:	J C Ulrich

30 mins. sound, b/w 35mm.
Première: Paris, Spring 1965.
The English version has a brief introduction by Bertrand Russell.

'Under what circumstances did you go to Vietnam?
I had been invited to go by Vietnamese film-makers I had met at various festivals – Moscow, Leipzig. Each time they repeated their invitation, but I was always too busy: Cuba, Chile, and *Le Mistral* above all took up a lot of my time. This summer I was free, and I went there for the month of July. The day after my arrival in Hanoi I went to the documentary film studios and talked to the artists and technicians there. I told them about the European cinema and our conditions of work, but then they said to me, "It's different here. Our cinema is very young. Look." And they explained to me that their cinema dated from 1954. They started off in 16mm, using cameras for amateurs left behind by French officers. I saw a projector which they had converted into a printer. I also saw the primitive methods they used for drying film. Nothing was mechanised. . . Once you realise that

then you realise that what they have done is remarkable. After two years they began to use their first 35mm camera and now they have a centre which employs about 250 people on the documentary and newsreel side, but their technology is very limited. For example, they only have one editing table for their *whole* production, fiction films included. So a real struggle goes on around that table. . . When I was filming there with a 16mm camera we only had very sensitive film. . . Since the light is so intense I said, "OK, let's use a grey filter". But I found out that they didn't have a grey filter in the whole studio, and had very few filters of any kind. . .And these are things that you can buy at a corner shop here, for four or five francs. And everything is like that. I talked to the director of the film archive: they had a few books, some films, but almost nothing. . . They had seen some Chinese, Soviet and Polish films. . . Flaherty was only a name to them. Of my own work they only had *Song of the Rivers* and *Die Windrose*. So you have to talk in a different way to young film-makers who have such primitive resources at their disposal. . . But they have what many don't have, an incredible revolutionary spirit. . .

Where does their equipment come from?
From just about everywhere. From China, from the GDR, the Soviet Union. They also have Arriflexes from West Germany, and Paillards. . . They have everything, but only a little of everything.

Do they also produce fiction films?
A few. Three or four a year, I believe. I was there such a short time that I couldn't see any. But they told me that since the war their fiction film-makers had mainly worked on documentaries and newsreels. There was the same phenomenon in the countries involved in the Second World War. In the Soviet Union, Pudovkin, Dovzhenko made documentaries as well. And in the United States, Capra and John Ford entered into the documentary service, as being more useful in the war effort. . . In Vietnam the cameramen are very active, they live with their cameras. What is weaker is the editing and the commentaries. They are aware of that, so I believe that that will improve too, but it is difficult, because you don't just learn editing from your colleagues – you have to watch other films and analyse them. . . All the same I was astonished by the quality of some sequences.

Tell us something about the film you are making.
. . . I brought back about 2,000 metres of 35mm, and 600 metres of 16mm since I had a camera of each type. . . I also asked for supplementary material, newsreels, documents on South Vietnam. At the moment in Paris I am actually in the process of editing all this. First of all I thought of making a kind of 'travel notebook', but then I decided to enlarge its scope. I have seen newsreels of the Front in the South here in Paris; and from time to time there have been some glimpses of the North; and US information services

have produced material. But this is never linked together, and I want to make a film which unites all this: the struggle of Buddhists in the South, the army which is preparing itself in the North, the Liberation Army in the South, the transformation of a guerrilla war into a real war, the enormous forces which the United States is putting into it, the peaceful work which goes on in the fields, everything, all Vietnam. A synthesis of a kind, which can give an exact idea of the situation in Vietnam. There is already great sympathy for Vietnam in France, and US aggression thousands of kilometres from its shores, draped with such hypocrisy, has few supporters. Then *Carnet de voyage* was just a working title, and I must find another which can translate what I want to show: Vietnam in war, the North, the South, the American point of view, that of the fighters, mine. I want to be informative, to tell the truth about the situation.

Have you brought back any recordings?
Unfortunately no. The equipment is both too bulky and too limited. Even fiction films there are post-synched. Vietnamese reporters use silent equipment and so did I. Tape recorders are mainly used for the radio. There was a small tape recorder which I used for my interview with Ho Chi Minh, but it was very bad, unusable, and I shall have to intervene, and say it all myself.

But I believe that the film itself isn't just intended to inform us about Vietnam, but also aims to help North Vietnamese film-makers?
Yes, that's true. The film is produced under unusual conditions. It's the same formula that I used in Spain in 1937 and in China in 1938. It's a non-commercial production. Nobody working on the film receives a wage: not myself, or the editor, the musical director, the narrator, or the writer etc. . . The producer will only take a small percentage to cover administrative costs. All the profit from this film will go towards helping film-makers in Vietnam: it will be transformed into cameras, filters, editing tables, film-stock.

You have also launched an appeal in different magazines.
Yes, I'm in the process of mounting a great campaign amongst film-makers in different countries to help their colleagues, to send them material, books, and so on. . . I believe that their struggle involves all of us and we must help them to have more efficient methods. I shall write to Buñuel, to Losey and to others, without forgetting the Americans, not all of whom are in favour of their government's policies towards Vietnam. I have already given interviews to *Le Monde* and *France Nouvelle* and I hope that other magazines will be prepared to participate in this campaign. Already Henri Storck, the Belgian film-maker, has given me an editing table for silent film, and other film-makers have written to me. . . Everyone can do something because they need everything: books, journals, accessories. . . The smallest thing

can be useful. That's why I'm asking everyone, and within a few months I hope to be able to say to the Vietnamese film-makers: Here's the equipment, the world is thinking about you.' (Joris Ivens, interview with Guy Gauthier, *Image et Son*, October 1965)

In 1965 Ivens was commissioned by the town council of Rotterdam to make a film about its port, the second most important for traffic after New York. This film, the first Ivens had made in Holland since *New Earth* in 1934, was a sign of his final re-acceptance into the history of Dutch cinema. As theme he chose to use the legend of the Flying Dutchman, condemned to sail around the world eternally unless he can find a woman who really loves him; rest will then come, but at the price of mortality.

1966: **Rotterdam-Europoort** (Rotterdam Europort) Holland

Producers:	Nederlandse Filmproduktie Mij, Rotterdam; Argos-Film, Paris
Director:	Joris Ivens
Assistant Directors:	Mirek Sebestik, Marceline Loridan
Camera:	Eduard Van der Enden, Etienne Becker
Editors:	Catherine Dourgnon, Geneviève Louveau, Andrée Choty
Music:	Pierre Barbot, Konstantin Simonovitch
Commentary:	written and spoken by Gerrit Kouwenaar; French narrator Yves Montand

20 mins. sound colour 35mm.
Première: Rotterdam, April 1966

'I imagined that the Flying Dutchman had chosen 1965 as the year to return to his home country and to see Rotterdam. He therefore had to use modern techniques. He no longer has his old boat, but a strange one instead, which occasionally, as it went at great speed, had things like paws or wings, like a crab or a spider. A small boat! And my Flying Dutchman is dressed in a James Bond way, in a frogman's suit. . . He isn't surprised by modern techniques. He admires them, he knows they are there. But of course he sees that something is missing from this technique: a human aspect, a social side is missing; there is something that isn't quite right. So I then had to deepen my perceptions of what I was seeing. This is a semi-documentary film, in part a fantasy. It is not an *Alphaville*; my film does not condemn technique. For example, the port of Rotterdam is very proud of the fact that any boat, of any kind, can enter it: big or small, powered by oars, sails, diesel or atomic fuel. All can enter, except one: that of the Flying Dutchman because he does not understand radar guidance. He has a compass, but this is useless because there are enormous stores of metal at Rotterdam, which stops any compass from functioning normally. His map is even from the eighteenth century, so cannot be any help. He can hear a radio signal, but what can he do?

62

'Later, we see the radar installations, visit the port, the docks, and even go to the Opera in Rotterdam, where, of course, they are performing *The Flying Dutchman*. And our Flying Dutchman walks in there, astonished himself, and astonishing others. At the end he leaves, just like the legend, despite a girl he meets at the Museum, after the Opera, where, of course, she plays the role of Sainta. "You are lovely," he says, "but the sea is calling to me, I cannot stay. . ." And he goes, a very fantastic departure, where I used CinemaScope to deform the image. And he is no longer dressed as a frogman, but as a pirate, with plumed hat and a torch, and he stands on his ship as if it were a horse. He sails towards the sun, and that's the end.' (Joris Ivens interviewed by Robert Grelier, *Positif*, June 1966)

Rotterdam-Europoort was the first film in which Marceline Loridan collaborated with Joris Ivens. Her introduction to cinema had been via friendship with Edgar Morin. Morin collaborated with Jean Rouch in the making of *Chronique d'un été* (1961), a classic of *cinéma vérité*. Marceline Loridan was one of the main participants in the film, and after this worked in television for some years. Her different formation and experience was to make a profound impact on Ivens' work in the following years. Now close collaborators in film, they are also married.

7 Politics and Cinema III: 1967–77

In the spring of 1967 Ivens returned to Vietnam and spent four months filming in North Vietnam, recording daily life in Hanoi and life in the regions close to the 17th Parallel, the point of troop demarcation and truce agreed upon at the Geneva Conference in 1954, after French defeat at the battle of Dien Bien Phu, which then became a *de facto* frontier between North and South.

The material on life in Hanoi was sent to Paris, together with a descriptive letter, both of which were used in the making of *Far From Vietnam*. This film, a gesture of solidarity by French film-makers to the Vietnamese in struggle against the US government, was the result of an initiative by Chris Marker, who edited all the material and whose film in some ways it really is.

1967: **Loin du Vietnam** (Far From Vietnam) France

Producer:	SLON
Production Organisers:	Jacqueline Meppiel, Andréa Haran
Directors' Collective:	Alain Resnais, Jean-Luc Godard, Joris Ivens, William Klein, Claude Lelouch, Agnès Varda
With the collaboration of:	Chris Marker, Michel Ray, Roger Pic, Marceline Loridan, François Maspéro, Jacques Sternberg, Jean Lacouture
Editor:	Chris Marker
Music:	Michel Fano, Michel Chapdenat, Georges Aperghis

Commentary: Maurice Garrel, Bernard Fresson, Karen
Bianguernon
115 mins. sound colour 35mm.
Première: Besançon, October 1967

Other material, on life close to the border with the South, became a new film, perhaps one of the best made on Vietnam, *The 17th Parallel,* Ivens' first film to be co-directed with Marceline Loridan. If her contribution to Ivens' work can be pinned to any one thing it would be sound. In contradistinction to Ivens' other directly political films, the major part of this (about 80%) is in Vietnamese, with subtitles. It represents a major shift.

1967: **Le dix-septième parallèle** (The 17th Parallel) Vietnam; France
Producers: CAPI-Films, Paris; Argos-Film Paris
Directors: Joris Ivens, Marceline Loridan
With the participation of: Bui Dinh Hac, Nguyen Thi, Xuan Phuong, Nguyen Quang Tuan, Dao Le Binh, Pham Chou, Liliane Korb, Maguy Alziari, Phuong Ba Tho, Jean-Pierre Sergent, Dang Voe Bich Lien, Jean Neny, Antoine Bonfanti, Pierre Angles, Michel Fano, Harald Maury, Donald Sturbelle, André Van der Beken, Bernard Ortion, Georges Loiseau; The Central Documentary Studios, Hanoi; the people of Vinh Linh
113 mins. sound b/w 35mm.
Première: Paris 6 March 1968, Studio Gît-le-Coeur

'The film is made for the Vietnamese, through them. This was only possible because we lived completely with the population, the peasants and soldiers, day and night. For two months we had the same shelter, the same food, the same weapons, the same enemy, the same danger. . .

How many were you in your team?
About ten: two Vietnamese camera operators, Marceline Loridan, a doctor-translator, assistants and production organisers. Marceline Loridan participated in everything, the film's conception, its construction. . . and one can say that about each of us. . .
Our translator-doctor was very precious to us; she knew how to translate feelings as much as language, and could arouse interest and enthusiasm for the cinema in the local population, and for their work in me. Thanks to her the film could perhaps be called a Vietnamese film. . .

Could the film be called a piece of testimony?
Le ciel, la terre is a testimony, and I wanted to do part of the commentary myself in order to give it more of an eye-witness quality. *17th Parallel* is a lived chronicle; it is no longer a question of making some very important generalisations, as in *Le ciel, la terre,* but of living the daily life of the village, which allowed us to understand very much more. . .

How long did the editing take?
More than four months. The editing posed some very difficult problems for the chief editor and myself: for example, the sequence where children are playing at capturing a pilot – I tried that out at the beginning, then in the middle, at the end and so on. It is linked to a theme of pilots which runs throughout the whole film, intermingled with other themes – of shelters, craters: craters representing the wounds the enemy inflicts on the earth, and at the same time the positive activity of the Vietnamese. They grip the earth, using it under all its forms, even the crater-form; they fill it in, grow sweet potatoes, raise fish. It is in that way that the film isn't sad, but positive. The war welded the people together; it's brought the best out of them.

You mentioned themes. Is the film constructed from certain themes?
No, I jumped into life, and reality made me a gift of some themes. To be a lived chronicle, a film should not be too constructed. But this isn't a question of making a naturalistic film. When there are burning issues you risk falling into pure reportage, into an actuality which rests on the surface without penetrating into life's values and truth. Sometimes there is a false glorification of authenticity. Authenticity is not the truth, but a factor in the truth. What guarantees truth is the integrity of the director, the confidence felt by people towards the camera and the director.

I attempted to make this in a different style from the rest of my work, less lyrical, almost an anonymous form. I foreswore everything I found easy. In this film there are no fades, no dissolves, no dynamic montage – and I am known for active editing. . .

I also, consciously, expelled all exotic content, even so far as suppressing palm trees when cutting the image to the right or left! In order to avoid all the exotic associations which there are for a French audience, so that your identification can be more direct without being restrained by the actions of your fathers and grandfathers. In *17th Parallel* aesthetic problems, even of framing, have an ideological content.' (Joris Ivens, Interview with Luce Sand, *Jeune Cinéma*, No. 30, April 1968, pp11–12)

17th Parallel marks a new change in direction for Ivens' work. Longer sequences begin to be used and there is less dramatic montage. Direct sound, too, comes to play a more important part in the construction of his films, no doubt as a result of Marceline Loridan's expertise. Their next film, made in Laos, makes these changes clear, and to a certain extent was related to criticism of *17th Parallel* and of one of Ivens' strengths – the emotional power of his work:

'*Marceline:* I want to add two things: on the one hand, when we went to Laos our level of political consciousness had grown, mainly from the fact of the development of struggles in Europe; on the other hand, I now find some aspects of *The 17th Parallel* inadequate: for example, it shows too many cadres and not enough of the masses, it doesn't let the people speak enough.

Didn't The 17th Parallel *appear a more concrete film to the ordinary spectator? Didn't it show more of what the people have concretely achieved?*

Joris: The audience could have the feeling that they are living with the Vietnamese in *The 17th Parallel.* And perhaps they will feel that less with *The People and their Guns*, but I believe that they will learn more from it, because of the treatment. In fact one could sit in an armchair in front of *The 17th Parallel* and, to a certain extent, 'enjoy' one's emotions. This isn't possible this time. You are forced to listen.

Marceline: The 17th Parallel plays a little on fascination. People came out of screenings saying 'What an extraordinary people.' . . . *The People and their Guns* shows more the organisational methods. In *The 17th Parallel,* for example, you only saw the military work of soldiers, and not their political work.

Joris: All the same, you shouldn't underestimate the film: it also leads people to reflect on the reasons for which the Vietnamese are winning the war.

Jean-Pierre: The 17th Parallel describes the level at which the Vietnamese people have arrived, shown by their actions. But something is lacking in the film: the statement of the conditions for reaching this stage. Nothing is said about the political work which preceded this and made these results possible. In summary, one could say that *Le ciel, la terre* is a poster, *17th Parallel* a narrative, *The People and Their Guns* an essay on theory.' (Joris Ivens, Marceline Loridan, Jean-Pierre Sergent, Interview in *Cinéma 70,* No. 143)

The People and their Guns, then, contains an element of active and conscious self-criticism. Shot in caves in Laos during 1968, it records the life of a liberated area. Whilst the film was being made news was heard via the BBC World Service of the events in Paris in May 1968 – red and black flags floating over the Odéon. On their return from Laos, Ivens and Loridan decided to link up with some of those who had participated in these events and form a new collective to complete the film. Many of the aesthetic arguments which were given a wider public through May '68 are present in the film. In particular the refusal of narrative and of visual pleasure.

1968–69: **Le peuple et ses fusils** (The People and their Guns) Laos; France
Producer: CAPI Films, Paris
Film Collective: Jean-Pierre Sergent, Marceline Loridan,
                              Joris Ivens, Emmanuele Castro, Suzanne Fenn,
                              Antoine Bonfanti, Bernard Ortion, Anne Rullier.
97 mins. sound b/w 35mm.
Première: 11 February 1970, Studio de la Harpe, Paris

The film was refused a licence for distribution outside France because it was interpreted by the Film Control Commission as a propaganda document, violently anti-American and hostile to the Laotian government. Nor was it allowed to be shown in French territories overseas.

'Why did you make a film collectively?'
From the moment we began work on the film we had to listen to, to study and analyse the political documents the leaders and cadres of the Laotian Patriotic Front gave us. It was starting from these discussions that little by little the choice of themes became elaborated, that's to say the subject of sequences. So it was already a collective work . . . When we returned, the need to pursue this work in common and at the same time to enlarge our collective was felt by everyone. Whilst we had been away there had been the May revolts, the general strike. This had to be taken into consideration. Our film was going to address itself to an audience which came fresh from the experience of a certain type of revolt and also a temporary setback to this revolt. That is why we worked with French militants.

Le peuple et ses fusils is different from the documentaries you usually make on similar subjects. It is unlike any of the films you have each made separately. You must have noticed this difference.
From the fact that, from beginning to end, we really worked together and collectively, the product of our work could not resemble anything which one of us could produce alone. Moreover, this proved to us how useful and fruitful collective work can be. Undoubtedly the specificity of this film lies essentially in the systematic application of those procedures required, we think, by the didactic position we took up. These procedures are a non-dramatic, fragmentary construction, the use of many more and much longer explanatory captions than are usually allowed, and so on.

In reality all film sequences are fragments. In this film they can be read as such. The explanatory captions accentuate even more the impression of discontinuity. They allow the spectator at every moment to achieve a distance in relation to what is being seen.

The spectator controls, criticises and can break free of the fascination effect which is often exercised by those authors who can ingeniously mask all lacunae, who can dramatise to the bitter end, who can play on subjectivity. . .

Throughout the film we see militants or soldiers in the process of trying to convince the peasants that they must participate in the struggle, give rice for the front, take up arms, etc. Don't you think this looks like propaganda?

No, because we realise the need for propaganda work. It is the word 'propaganda' which is the obstacle. Obviously American reactionaries will be very happy to recognise their famous 'brain-washing' here. Laotian revolutionaries very properly call it the work of explanation and persuasion. And they know to what extent this work is irreplaceable. In a country of poor peasants, where ethnic and linguistic divisions have been systematically aggravated by colonialism and puppet governments, there are many false ideas which must be rooted out from people's heads.

We show very well that the people are not passive. This work of explanation and persuasion is one of apprenticeship in the revolution, where everyone learns: the people from the militants, but also the militants from the people . . .

This word 'propaganda' offends because bourgeois ideology has invested it with pejorative meaning. But we ourselves do not make these semantic slippages of the bourgeoisie. We reply to the bourgeoisie in our own language, our language as revolutionaries. In this sense our film is a propaganda film: we have seen, understood and proved that a People's War of Liberation is a school of ideological revolutionisation. And we want that to become known.' (Joris Ivens: *Cinéma Politique*, Special Issue on Joris Ivens, November 1978, pp70-71)

The next film, *Rencontre avec le Président Ho Chi Minh*, is very much in the same style, eschewing montage, and depicting a conversation between Pham Van Dong, the Prime Minister of North Vietnam, Ho Chi Minh, and Vietnamese activists from North and South Vietnam, all sitting round a table. The film emerges as if it were a single sequence shot.

1969: **Rencontre ave le Président Ho Chi Minh** (Meeting with President Ho Chi Minh) Vietnam; France
Producer: CAPI Films, Paris
Directors: Joris Ivens, Marceline Loridan
8 mins. sound colour 35mm.
Premiére: Paris, 11 March 1970, Studio de la Harpe

Ivens' and Loridan's next project turned out to be monumental one. Starting in 1971, they began work on a film on everyday life in China. Originally planned to be a four-hour film showing life in China in 1973, shooting and editing went on into 1975 and the material became a series of films, twelve hours in all. This film cycle, *How Yukong Moved the Mountains*, was financed partly by the French Centre National du Cinéma, and partly by the instruction Ivens and Loridan gave to Chinese technicians in camera and sound in the course of filming. *Yukong* has been widely shown, on TV as well as in cinemas, and brought the attention of a new audience to Ivens' documentary career.

1971-75: **Comment Yukong déplaça les montagnes** (How Yukong Moved the Mountains) China; France
Producers: CAPI Films, Paris; Institut National de l'Audio-

	Visuel (L'INA), Paris
Directors:	Joris Ivens, Marceline Loridan, with the collaboration of Jean Bigiaoui (Editor)
Camera:	Li Tse-Hsieng
Assistant Camera:	Yang Tse Zu
Production assistants:	Zu Choung-Yuan, Tchen Li-Jen, Ye Che-Choun
Filming assistant:	Wou Mung-Ping
Lighting electrician:	Tia Chiao-He
Assistant:	Kao We-Tien
Translators in China and France:	Ho Tien, Lu Sung-He, Tan Kien-Wen, Yam Cheng
Chief editors:	Suzanne Baron, Sylvie Blanc, Eric Pluet, Ragnard Van Leyden
Assistant Editors:	Joëlle Dalido, Sarah Matton
Sound Editing:	Paul Bertault, Joël Beldent
Commentary:	with the collaboration of Alain Badiou
Dubbing:	Jacques Lévy, Jacques Sansoulh, Alain Landau, with help from Lucien Logette, Julie Vilmont, Dominique Valenteur
Cartography:	Renée Koch

12 hours sound colour 16mm.
Première: Paris, 10 March 1976

The film is in 12 parts:
1. The Oilfields: Ta Ching (84 mins.)
2. The Pharmacy: Shanghai (79 mins.)
3. The Generator Factory (131 mins.)
4. A Woman, A Family (110 mins.)
5. The Fishing Village (104 mins.)
6. An Army Camp (56 mins.)
7. Impressions of a City: Shanghai (60 mins.)
8. The Football Incident (19 mins.)
9. Professor Tsien (12 mins.)
10. Rehearsal at the Peking Opera (30 mins.)
11. Training at the Peking Circus (18 mins.)
12. Traditional Handicrafts (15 mins.)

'Joris and Marceline, you have just spent some months in the People's Republic of China. According to what we have read in Pékin Informations *and the Chinese Press Agency Hsin-Hua, your film* Comment Yukong déplaça les montagnes *has been shown and discussed there. What reception did it have, who criticised it and who approved of it?*
ML: To begin with, the film was shown to people we filmed. Afterwards there were official screenings. There was also a screening at the French Embassy, to which all the ambassadors accredited to Peking came.

Did your film provoke different reactions from the officials and from the Chinese?
ML: Curiously, reactions were almost always the same. The ambassadors were sometimes sorry to see that our films were so close to the reality of everyday life in China, from which they were so removed. Naturally, they had never been able to spend four months in a factory. The people we filmed were very excited. They had long discussions after the screening and told us that when we were shooting they had not been able to tell to what extent the films could be interesting. A worker in the generator factory told us at the end of one session that when we started to film he said to himself: 'These are foreigners who would not come to see us unless they were filming us'. After a few days of filming, when he had seen that we filmed people and not machines, he said to himself: 'Perhaps this could be an interesting film'.

We also showed the workers the raw material, developed, but not yet edited and without sound, and at that time they wanted to know: 'What can you do with that, it will be terribly boring!' Then, when we showed the finished film, people said: 'But it's our everyday life, which we know by heart. That's boring.' The day after they telephoned us and said that they had thought about the film all night, that the film had really bowled them over. They didn't know for what reason, they said, because they hadn't seen anything but their own life.

JI: The films were very interesting for Chinese film-makers, because they themselves, for different reasons, had so far worked very little with synchronised sound. Partly for technical reasons, and also partly because of the cultural dictatorship exercised by Madame Chiang Ching. During that period the seven approved models of opera were, to tell the truth, the only way of making films or operas.

And suddenly here was a film which did the opposite, which let the people speak. I still remember very well, for example, talking about my plans to Chou En-Lai, who said: 'Yes, now I understand. You let the people speak.' It is very important that in this film it isn't me or Marceline who does the talking but that 80% of it is the Chinese people. We also had numerous discussions with documentarists – for example, about collaboration between sound and camera. They were still at the stage of the silent camera there – with musical accompaniment – in the rice fields there was always the same music – and a commentator who knew everything. That's the reason why our films are now used as study material at the film school. We have even heard those who make fiction films say: 'Sometimes the workers are better actors than we are.' I say yes and no. The workers have the power to represent their own reality, but you must also add other feelings, some delicacy. This means that you have to work with them. Chinese film-makers will never really end up imagining that workers can talk in front of the camera with such naturalness and such assurance.

Whilst you were filming did you feel the cultural dictatorship of those who are called the 'gang of four'?
JI: No. It was essentially Chinese film-makers who felt the cultural dictatorship. But I can easily imagine that if we had made the film two years later, in 1975/76, we would also have felt that pressure directly. When we returned to China to film some additional sections we noticed that people were not so free. Sometimes, as well, we weren't able to get information. During these two years the influence of these four people became much more aggressive, stronger.

Can your films be seen in Chinese cinemas?

JI: The Chinese version, which is really our international version, is now shown in many cinemas in many towns.' (Joris Ivens and Marceline Loridan, Interview with Alexandra Kluge and Bion Steinborn, *Filmfaust*, May 1977)

Out of this work in China came two other films, not yet released in Britain, on the life of national minorities in Sinkiang.

1973-77: **Les Kazaks — minorité nationale — Sinkiang** China; France
Producer: C A P I Films, Paris

Directors: Joris Ivens, Marceline Loridan
Editor: Suzanne Baron
50 mins. sound colour 16mm.

1973-77: Les Ouigours – minorité nationale — Sinkiang China; France
Producer: CAPI Films, Paris
Directors: Joris Ivens, Marceline Loridan
Editor: Suzanne Baron
35 mins. sound colour 16mm.

In 1978 Joris Ivens celebrated his eightieth birthday and fifty years of film-making. A complete retrospective of his work was organised at the Filmmuseum in Amsterdam, where he had deposited his personal archive in 1969. A travelling exhibition was also designed. During 1979 there were retrospectives in the United States at the Museum of Modern Art in New York, in Italy at Modena, in Paris at the Cinémathèque, and at the National Film Theatre in London. The exhibition has been shown in Italy, France and Britain.

Film commentaries

Extract from Spanish Earth Commentary

When Ivens went to America it was at a time of growth of new documentary genres: documentary reportage with photographs (*Let Us Now Praise Famous Men,* by Agee and Evans, is one example), the documentary novel (John Dos Passos, *USA* amongst others), and the development of 'participant observation' in sociology (Whyte's *Street Corner Society* came from research started in 1936). This is not an all-inclusive list of genres, but an indication of the multiple forms a documentary orientation took. Hemingway's work was within this documentary movement, and he himself acted as a reporter. One aspect of this movement was an interest in conveying not just the facts about an experience or situation, but also how it felt: documentary was thus a means of sharing experience. *Spanish Earth* can be understood as a fusion between the documentary methods Ivens had been developing in Europe and the American forms.

This is an edited version of the commentary of *The Spanish Earth,* written by Hemingway, who was also part of the film crew, and spoken by him in the final version of the film. The narrator acts as bridge between the screen and the spectator; what is interesting in this commentary is the various shifts in position of the narrator. At times he is identified with the peasants on screen, speaking on their behalf – 'they held us back'; at times gives information – 'the village is on the Tagus River'; at times explains feeling – 'each man knows there is only himself'; at times identifies with the audience – 'They say the old goodbyes that sound the same in any language'. A careful look at this commentary shows that it is not one position which is occupied, but rather that its strength comes from a multiplicity of forms of address. The commentary is also marked by a strong internal speech-rhythm. The screen image is taken as point of departure, so that there is no narrative drive, only the movement of associations.

'This Spanish Earth is dry and hard and the faces of the men that work the earth are dry and hard from the sun. This worthless land, with water will yield much. For fifty years we've wanted to irrigate, but they held us back. Now we will bring water to it to raise food for the defenders of Madrid.

The village of Fuentaduena where 1,500 people live and work the land for the common good. It is good bread, stamped with the union label, but there is only enough for the village. Irrigating the wasteland of the village gives ten times as much grain for bread, as well as potatoes, wine, and onions for Madrid. The village is on the Tagus river and the main high road is the lifeline between Valencia and Madrid. All food from the village comes on this road. To win the war the rebel troops must have this road.

They plan the irrigation of the dry fields. They go to trace the ditch.

This is the true face of men going into action. There is little difference from any other faces you will ever see. Men cannot act before the camera in the presence of death [. . .]

When you are fighting to defend your country – war as it is now becomes an almost normal life. You eat and drink and read the papers [. . .]

When these men started for the lines three months ago many of them held a rifle for the first time. Some did not even know how to reload. Now they are instructing the new recruits how to take down and reassemble a rifle [. . .]

Living in the cellars of that ruined building are the enemy. They are Moors and pinned down. They are brave troops or they would not have held out after their position was hopeless. But they are professional soldiers fighting against the people in arms, trying to impose the will of the military on the will of the people and the people hate them, for without their tenacity and the constant aid of Italy and Germany the Spanish revolt would have ended six weeks after it began [. . .]

Madrid by its position is a natural fortress and each day the people make its defences more impregnable.

You stand in line all day to buy food for supper. Sometimes the food runs out before you reach the door, sometimes a shell falls near the line and at home they wait and wait and no one brings back anything for supper. Unable to enter the town the enemy tries to destroy it.

This is a man who had nothing to do with the war, a book-keeper on the way to his office at 8 o'clock in the morning. So now they take the book-keeper away, but neither to his home or to his office.

The government urges all citizens to evacuate Madrid. But where will we go? Where can we live? What can we do for a living? I won't go. I'm too old.

We must keep the children off the streets except when they need to stand in line [. . .]

They say the old goodbyes that sound the same in any language. She says she'll wait. He says that he'll come back. He knows she'll wait. Who knows for what the way the shelling is. Nobody knows if he'll come back. Take care of the kid, he says. I will, she says, and knows she can't. They both know that when they move you out in trucks it's to a battle.

Death comes each morning to these people in the town. Sent by the rebels from the hills two miles away. The smell of death is acrid high explosive smoke and blasted granite. Why do they stay? They stay because this is their city; these are their homes; here is their work. This is their fight. The fight to be allowed to live as human beings.

74

The men move on in columns of six in the ultimate loneliness of what is known as combat. For each man knows there is only himself and five other men and before them all the great unknown. This is the moment that all the rest of the war prepares for. When six men go forward into death, to walk across a stretch of land and by their presence on it prove this earth is ours.

The counter-attack has been successful. The road is free. Six men were five, then four were three. But these three stayed, dug in and held the ground. Along with all the other fours and threes and twos that started out as sixes.

The Bridge is ours. The road is saved. The men who never fought before, who were not trained in arms, who only wanted work and food, fight on.

Song of the Rivers

> *Song of the Rivers* was commended for its 'universalism', and this edited version is designed to foreground the universalistic features of Vladimir Pozner's commentary. It should be pointed out, however, that the English version is not in all places an exact translation of the original, which starts, for example, by commenting on the beauty of nature. The unity which is created in the film, by word and image, is that of the composite worker, labouring to transform nature through machinery and to create a better world – 'if it was up to us'. The composite worker of the commentary thus speaks to the audience directly, setting up a dialogue, which also takes place within the film – 'All my life I've been hungry'. The second-person form is used usually to address elements of the film material – the Statue of Liberty, Pharoah, oppressed African workers – and only rarely used to the audience – 'Do you remember her? Aye, Stalingrad'. The voice also, impersonally, is giver of information, 'The land is not theirs yet', recording history and modes of exploitation. It is a more static commentary than that of Hemingway, designed to build up the sense of the seventh river of the film: that of a vast, internationally organised and internationally relevant workers' movement, which one day will be the master.

Aye, but man can yet be the master. By the power of his strong right arm and his intelligence. He obeys me like a little child. Tomorrow it will be a river. Yestday it was a desert. We built all this. All of us together.

If it was up to us no-one in the world would be hungry. We'll make ships, houses, workshops, out of this forest. If it was up to us no-one would be without a home. We built it. All of us together. If it was up to us no-one in the world would be cold. Workers, all of us, we create all the wealth of the world. Day by day with our hands, yellow, white or black, we change the face of the earth and the future of mankind.

(Song by Semion Kirsanov, sung in English)

If it was up to us man would be happy.
Happy? Happy? All my life I've been hungry. I sleep in the streets. It hurts. I expect nothing more of life. Where we live people die before they reach thirty. I have eight years to live.

Water is precious. A rusty old drum even more precious. Only men are cheap. They're much cheaper than machines. And no upkeep . . .

. . . Take a look at what's happening behind your back. See how thousands of your sons have to live. (addressed to the Statue of Liberty)

You remember how beautiful this country was. The Indians called it the father of the waters. The Mississippi.

On the banks of the Mississippi wheat and cotton grow, but not to feed and clothe the poor. The factories make money, not happiness.

On the banks of the Mississippi the poor work for the rich and when they're black they're twice as poor and work twice as hard. And to keep the Negroes in their place . . . The Klu Klux Klan. The American way of death.

To master the Mississippi for good would take less money than the United States spends each year to prepare for war.

(Brecht song: the Mississippi verse)

The peoples of India call her mother. Mother Ganges.

On the banks of the Ganges there are two harvests each year. On the banks of the Ganges 200 years ago British merchants set up shop. On the banks of the Ganges every day men die of hunger. They grew up under British rule like their father and grandfathers before them. Two centuries of foreign rule. Two centuries of famine. 400 harvests, 2 a year, so that the bankers of London, Paris and New York should never run short of profits.

The people who built a great civilisation could never remain in slavery. The Ganges is an Indian river once more. There are no foreign troops in Calcutta. But there are still foreign business men.

On the banks of the Ganges workers spin cotton for others. On the banks of the Ganges there are two crops a year and harvest time is coming.

(Brecht song: the Ganges verse)

5,000 years ago the Egyptians called the Nile the father of the Gods. Here where a river and a people came together the oldest civilisation of all was born. In their day they used to say 'we get up early every day to suffer'. And today the peasant rises early. The same motion, the same toil.

What are you gazing at Pharoah? At men who build as my slaves built. What can you see? Men toiling as they toiled in my time.

On the banks of the Nile the peasants rise early to suffer. A modern dam? Yes. But the peasants still rise before dawn.

Nothing makes a land blossom like the waters of a river and the sweat of a people. From dawn to dusk harvesting cotton. The profits are harvested in London, Amsterdam, New York.

The Egyptians struggle to make the Nile an Egyptian river again. The cotton kings sent troops to Egypt, they sent warships to Egypt. But the Nile would not change her course. Nor would history. The cotton kings are still the masters of Cairo.

On the banks of the Nile the workers get up early to suffer. They look obedient, they look calm, as calm as their Nile.

(Brecht song: the Nile verse)

India is on the road to independence, Egypt struggles for hers, but in Africa white men still rule over 210 million coloured men.

Cape Town. They export coffee, cocoa, rubber. They export wood, spices, groundnuts. They export gold, diamonds, uranium.

Good enough for black men.

Western civilisation shines upon the colonial world. Disease stalks the continent. Nigeria – half the children die before they're five. An African colony – 95 per cent of the children without schools.

Salt. Men die young at this work. The salt has eaten his legs.

It can't go on like this. You're workers. You've a right to have machines, to rest. You've a right to be happy. Brothers, listen to the call of the World

Federation of Trade Unions. Your lives become harder and harder. You can put an end to colonial slavery.

No, not convicts, workers in a colony.

Brothers, we live in different countries, we speak different languages, but we have common interests, for we belong to the same class . . .

. . . The World Federation of Trade Unions is organising a big Congress. The whole world will know how we live. How they beat us on their farms. How they send us to fight their wars. How we need tractors and machines and equipment. How we need schools and hospitals.

Who's in favour of sending a delegate to the Congress? They're coming from everywhere. Black, white, equal pay for equal work. We'll send a brother to the meeting in Europe to find out what the other organised workers are doing and we'll tell them what we're doing here in Africa . . .

. . . Chinese earth, Chinese peasants. Yesterday *they* owned everything. Yesterday *she* owned nothing.

Peasants of China, look at this land with a master's eye, for you are the master.

In the old days on the Yangtse human life was held so cheap that no-one bothered to count the dead or even the living. For a thousand years the Yangtse carried famine, pestilence, misery. Today the river is ours. The river must take its orders from us.

When you're an old man you'll be able to say 'I was there'. Soviet machinery was there too. And the river takes its orders. And here are the masters of the rivers and the harvests. Here are the masters. Aye, here are the masters.

Today the Yangtse carries lorries from Gorki and tractors from Stalingrad. New factories are going up on the banks of the Yangtse. Trade Union rest homes on the banks of the Yangtse.

There are 600,000,000 people in the new China. They took the count themselves for the first time because today nothing is more precious on the banks of the Yangtse than people.

(Brecht song: the Yangtse verse)

(. . .)

The Russians call her mother. Mother Volga.

Yes, here she is on the banks, in the sunlight. Do you remember her? Aye, Stalingrad. And this is the new Stalingrad.

Yesterday a desert, today a sea. Here men and river are friends. On the banks of the Volga men give their orders to machines. On the banks of the Volga man no longer struggles for his daily bread. He just brings in the harvest.

(Song by Semion Kirsanov, sung in Russian)

On the banks of the Volga, life is as good as bread and as beautiful as roses.

(Brecht song: the Volga verse)

The Amazon. The Indians call the Amazon the destroyer of boats.

These hands could assemble a chronometer or a turbine, but by this fire, history has slept for 20,000 years.

The land is not theirs yet. Nor are the towns. On the banks of the Amazon there are American businessmen, and the smell of petrol. Whose petrol? Standard Oil.

(Brecht song: the Amazon verse)

La Seine a rencontré Paris

by Jacques Prévert

The commentaries in Ivens' films are never simply descriptive
reinforcements of the image, and his use of montage usually operates
according to a chain of associations. This is particularly open in his
'film-poem', *La Seine a rencontré Paris*, where different aspects of the
river from town to countryside are counterpointed by Prévert's poem.
This poem is itself constructed as a chain of associations, through the
different meanings the river can have for a child, a lover, a jaded
tourist and so on, as well as for the poet himself.

Qui est là
toujours là dans la ville
et qui pourtant sans cesse arrive
et qui pourtant sans cesse s'en va

C'est un fleuve répond un enfant
un devineur de devinettes
Et puis l'oeil brillant il ajoute
Et le fleuve s'appelle la Seine
quand la ville s'appelle Paris
et la Seine c'est comme une personne
des fois elle court elle va très vite
   elle presse le pas quand tombe le soir
Des fois au printemps elle s'arrête et
   vous regarde comme un miroir
Et elle pleure si vous pleurez
ou sourit pour vous consoler
et toujours elle éclate de rire quand
   arrive le soleil d'été.

Who's there
always there in the city
and yet always coming
and always going

It's a river answers a child
that unriddles riddles
And then with sparkling eye he adds
And the river is called the Seine
while the city is called Paris
And the Seine is like a person
sometimes she runs and rushes past
        hurries her step when evening falls
Sometimes in spring she pulls up short and
        gazes at you like a mirror
And if you cry she cries
or smiles to cheer you up
and always breaks into laughter when
        the summer sun appears

81

La Seine dit un chat
c'est une chatte
elle ronronne en me frôlant
Ou peut-être que c'est une souris
qui joue avec moi puis s'enfuit

La Seine c'est une belle fille de dans le temps
une jolie fille du French Cancan
dit un très vieil Old Man River
un gentleman de la misère
et dans l'écume du sillage d'un lui
    aussi très vieux chaland
il retrouve les galantes images
du bon vieux temps tout froufroutant

La Seine
dit un manoeuvre
un homme de peine de rêves de muscles et de sueur
La Seine c'est une usine
la Seine c'est le labeur
En amont en aval toujours la même manivelle
Des fortunes de pinard de charbon et de blé
qui remontent et descendent le fleuve en suivant
    le cours de la Bourse
des fortunes de bouteilles et de verre brisé
des trésors de ferraille rouillée
de vieux lits cages abandonnés
ré-cu-pé-rés
La Seine
c'est une usine
même quand c'est la fraîcheur
c'est toujours le labeur

C'est une chanson qui coule de source
elle a la voix de la jeunesse
dit une amoureuse en souriant
une amoureuse du Vert-Galant
Une amoureuse de l'île des Cygnes
se dit la même chose en rêvant

La Seine
je la connais comme si je l'avais faite
dit un pilote de remorqueur au bleu de chauffe
    tout bariolé
tout bariolé de mazout et de soleil et de fumée

The Seine a tom-cat says
is a she-cat
who purrs and brushes past me
or perhaps a mouse
who toys with me and then runs off

The Seine is a fine girl of bygone days
a pretty French Cancan girl
says a very old Old Man River
a gentleman of poverty
and in the froth of the wash
        of an equally aging barge
he discovers an image that rustles
with the charm of the old days

The Seine
says a labourer
a man of sorrows of dreams of muscles and sweat
The Seine is a factory
the Seine is work
Upstream and down always the same turning handle
fortunes in wine in coal and wheat
which rise and fall with the river
        according to the tide of the market
fortunes in bottles and broken glass
treasure troves of rusted scrap
of old bedsteads abandoned
re-claimed
The Seine
is a factory
even when the weather's fresh
it's always work

It's a song from the headsprings
it has the voice of youth
says a woman in love from the Vert-Galant
as she smiles
A woman in love from the Ile des Cygnes
telling herself the same in her dreams

The Seine
I know her as if I'd made her myself
says a tug-boat pilot
        in a stained boiler-suit
streaked with oil and sun and smoke

Un jour elle est folle de son corps
elle appelle ça le mascaret
le lendemain elle roupille comme un loir
et c'est tout comme un parquet bien briqué
Scabreuse dangereuse tumultueuse et rêveuse
par-dessus le marché
voilà comment qu'elle est
Malice caresse romance tendresse caprice
vacherie paresse
Si ça vous intéresse c'est son vrai pedigree.

La Seine
C'est un fleuve comme un autre
et d'une voix désabusée un monsieur correct et blasé
Un des tout premier passager du grand tout dernier
bateau-mouche touristique et pasteurisé
Un fleuve avec des ponts des docks des quais
Un fleuve avec des remous des égouts et de temps à autre
un noyé
quand ce n'est pas un chien crevé
avec des pêcheurs à la ligne
et qui n'attrapent rien jamais
Un fleuve comme un autre comme un autre comme un autre

Et la Seine qui l'entend sourit
et puis s'éloigne en chatonnant

Un fleuve comme un autre comme un autre comme un autre
Un cours d'eau comme un autre cours d'eau
d'eau des glaciers et des torrents
et des lacs souterrains et des neiges fondues
des nuages disparus
Un fleuve comme un autre
comme la Durance ou le Guadalquivir
ou l'Amazone ou la Moselle
le Rhin la Tamise ou le Nil
Un fleuve comme le fleuve Amour
Comme le fleuve Amour
chante la Seine épanouie
et la nuit la voie lactée l'accompagne de sa tendre
rumeur dorée
et aussi la voie ferrée de son doux fracas coutumier

One day she flaunts her body
she calls it her tidal wave
the next she snoozes like a dormouse
and then she's just like a well-scrubbed floor
risky dangerous all over the place and dreamy
all at once
that's the way she is
Malice caress romance tenderness caprice
        bitchiness idleness
If you must know that's her real pedigree

The Seine
is a river like any other
says a monsieur with a disabused and blasé voice
one of the very first passengers of the very latest
        sterilised pleasure-boats for tourists
a river with bridges docks and quays
A river with eddies from sewers and
        occasionally a drowned man
when it isn't a dead dog
with anglers at their lines
who never catch a thing
a river like any other any other any other

And the Seine hears smiles
and slips away like a cat

A river like any other any other any other
a waterway like any other waterway
water from glaciers and torrents
and underground lakes and melted snow
and vanished clouds
A river like any other
like the Durance or the Guadalquivir
or the Amazon or Moselle
the Rhine the Thames or the Nile
A river like the river Love
Like the River Love
sings the broadening Seine
and at night the milky way accompanies its tender
        golden murmur
and also the railway with its usual muffled din

Comme le fleuve Amour
vous l'entendez la belle
vous l'entendez roucouler
dit un grand seigneur des berges
un estivant du quai de la Rapée
le fleuve Amour
tu parles si je m'en balance
c'est pas un fleuve la Seine
c'est l'amour en personne
c'est ma rivière à moi
mon petit point du jour
mon petit tour du monde
les vacances de ma vie

Et le Louvre avec les Tuileries la Tour Eiffel la Tour
    Pointue et Notre-Dame et l'Obélisque
La gare de Lyon ou d'Austerlitz
c'est mes châteaux de la Loire
la Seine
c'est ma Riviera
et moi je suis son vrai touriste
Et quand elle coule froide et nue en hurlant plainte
    contre inconnu
faudrait que j'aie mauvaise mémoire
pour l'appeler détresse misère ou désespoir

Faut tout de même pas confondre les contes de fées et les
    cauchemars
Aussi
quand dessous le Pont Neuf le vent du dernier jour soufflera
    ma bougie
quand je me retirerai des affaires de la vie
quand je serai définitivement à mon aise
au grand palace des allongés
à Bagneux au Père-Lachaise
je sourirai et me dirai
il était une fois la Seine
il était une fois
il était une fois l'amour
il était une fois le malheur
et une autre fois l'oubli

il était une fois la Seine
il était une fois la vie.

Like the river Love
Do you hear the beauty
Do you hear the cooing
says a lord of the barges
a summer visitor on the Rapée quay
the river Love
I can tell you I ride it
it isn't a river the Seine
it's love in person
it's my river
my little daybreak
my little trip round the world
my life's holidays

And the Louvre with the Tuileries the Eiffel and Pointue
        Towers and Notre-Dame and the Obelisk
The Gare de Lyon or the Austerlitz
it's my chateaux of the Loire
the Seine
it's my Riviera
and me I'm its true tourist
and when it runs cold and naked howling complaint
        against strangers
You have to be short on memory
to call it distress misery or despair

All the same mustn't confuse fairy tales
        and nightmares
And then
when below the Pont Neuf the dying day's wind blows out
        my candle
when I withdraw from the business of life
when I'm finally at ease
in the grand palace of those at rest
at Bagneux at Père-Lachaise
I shall smile and say to myself
there was once the Seine
once
there once was love
there was once misfortune
and another time forgetfulness

there was once the Seine
and once there was life.   (translated by Michael Chanan)

. . . A Valparaiso

This is the script based on the final editing of . . . A *Valparaiso*. It gives an impression of Ivens' active editing style, and of the relation set up between image and word. Once more the voice-over narrative informs the spectator, reflecting too on the significance of the images. The elements of the city and its life – hills, sea, wind, blood – emerge and are thrown back and forth from eye to ear.

The use of the first-person plural is different here from *Spanish Earth* and *Song of the Rivers*. When it refers to the needs of the people of Valparaiso, it is they who use it. In the mouth of the narrator it refers only to the experience of the audience – 'we played at pirates' – or, more exactly, to the audience's fantasies. The place of fantasy is signalled at the start of the film. 'Nous irons à Valparaiso', with its sea-shanty flavour, is a French children's song.

There is sometimes too strict a division made between Ivens the poet and Ivens the political realist. In this film Marker's evocative commentary and Ivens's imagery combine in a film which plays with poetic fantasy but whose politics are always present and available.

Opening shots of waves breaking on the rocks with the sound of thunder. A ship moves through the mist. A radar transmitter turns at the mast-head.

(*Voice-over*) Still two hours out of Valparaiso.

Close-up of radar panel as its luminous sights take in the coast line. The ship outlined in silhouette against the harbour. A master shot with everything lost in the evening mist. Close-up of a hand lighting a firework. The harbour and the ships are brilliantly lit by flare after flare of the display, while the music of the opening song softly rises.

The quaysides are a solid mass of people, intermittently lit by the beam from the lighthouse. A ship's propeller. On the quayside two children light a firework which burns out. At the foot of a lighthouse beacon some children climbing a stair, then a pan up towards the sky. Low-angle shot of a crane unloading a crate.

SONG*

Hardi, les gars, vire au gindeau (*Hurrah me bullies, heave the capstan O*)
Good bye, farewell, good bye, farewell
Adieu misère, adieu bateau (*Goodbye to the drudgery, goodbye to the ship*)
Hourra, oh Mexico.

On the quayside dockers lift bales from an unloading platform. Low-angle shot of a stairway rising up towards the heights of the town. A man carrying a crate. A shot from inside a lift lets us take in the view as we make the ascent from the harbour to the hills.

The port is down there.

*Translation of the song is based on the English version of it and is taken from *Shanties from the Seven Seas* by Stan Hugill, RKP (London) and E P Dutton and Co. (New York), 1961, p.129.

88

It was the richest port of all. It was the end of the voyage. It was where the ships put in. There were many songs about it.

A snip of the scissors in Panama put it back in its place, in the farthest-flung corner of the Pacific.

It is still a port. Valparaiso, Chile, population 300,000, between the Cordillera and the ocean. Not the richest, but it lives. It lives well. Beside it, down there at the foot of the hills, is the life of a commercial town.

Up on the hills there lives another town. Not a town: a federation of villages, one to each hill. Forty-two hills, forty-two villages. Not another town; another world.

Two worlds connected by ramps, stairs, lifts.

Master-shot of a lift-shaft, with a pan moving to another shaft in close-up. Inside the lift-cage passengers are sitting on wooden seats. A man, some elderly women, two young girls.

A stairway shot from very high up, from what looks like a vertical angle. Some children are sliding down the hand-rail. We follow them in a downward pan. Master-shot of stairs snaking down the hill-side. We follow a young girl as she walks down the steps. Another stairway alongside some houses. A lift takes us up to the top of a hill. As we go up we catch an unexpected glimpse of the lives people live inside the houses. Mid-shot of the lift cables.

All the way up a sloping street there are kids, and women sitting on the pavement. We pass under a bridge on the slope of one of the ramps. Further down we follow two horse-drawn hearses as far as the cemetery. Various shots of graves.

The word pronounced so dreadfully in French as Valparaiso is Val Para-iso, the Valley of Paradise. For the sailors who gave it its name it was the Paradise of a stretch of sunlight after the nightmares of the crossing. Or else the last stretch *before* Paradise.

The same leitmotiv of the lift cables passing in front of the camera (this will punctuate the images over and over again).

From behind an iron gate we follow a woman carrying a sunshade. At the bottom of a stairway a woman with her sunshade under her arm lifts a penguin in her arms. The next shot shows her putting it down and giving it a push with the end of her sunshade.

In this city, every day at noon the sun performs its wonders. All the women in Valparaiso come out with their sunshades to walk with all the penguins in Valparaiso.

A bridge shot against the sky from a low angle. High-angle shot of a triangular house on a corner where two streets intersect. On a hillside just below some houses a stairway comes to an abrupt end. A young girl goes down the steps and looks down.

The bridges all end up in the sky. The houses are all triangular and impossible to furnish. The stairways all stop half-way up the hill. Either you turn back or you fly.

A slow pan sweeps over a poor street with a tangle of electric wires overhead. A lift starts up. A lorry goes by in the foreground, revealing the shanty-dwellings sunlit on the hillside. Master-shot of a stairway.

In the sun poverty stops looking like poverty. The lifts stop looking like lifts.

This is the lie of Valparaiso. Its lie is the sun. Its truth is the sea.

Master-shot of the harbour: ships lie at anchor. Gulls glide in the sky overhead. On one quay a Diesel train is being unloaded. A few shots to show the work of the men as they manoeuvre it onto the rails.

Some other men are putting a ship's rudder in place. One man is hoisting; the man in charge is guiding his movements.

In an avenue of the city the name-plate of the Bank of London. A tram goes past in the foreground. A shot of a triumphal arch and a low-angle shot of a pedestal with the statue of a lion. A group of people with a Salvation Army member singing in their midst; pan to reveal a man lying on the pavement. A huge hoarding advertising women's underwear towers over the buildings: 'Bien-Jolie' and the name-plate of the Alliance Française cultural centre.

Founded, built and populated by sailors. Here the traces are English: the Bank of London and South America, the triumphal archways, the emblem of the lion, the Salvation Army and a cheap brand of whisky perhaps. To the New World France has offered the gallantry of its pirates and the last of its secret societies, the Alliance Française.

The centre of the city, with the building of the Spanish consortium and the teeming avenues jammed with buses. In one street a house with Moorish-style architecture and the hotel 'Singapur' by the entrance to a lift. A woman on the balcony of a well-to-do house ornamented with pilasters, reminding one of the commander on the bridge of a ship – and we catch sight of a triangular house with a balcony at the top, giving it the air of a ship's prow.

The Spanish baptised the city. They converted it, they adopted it, they married it. It betrayed them with the Dutch. The infidelity continues.

But all the sea-faring nations have left something to be remembered by. You find the same things that you find in the homes of the sailors, a souvenir of Casablanca, a souvenir of Singapore. How many houses have so much become memories of ships to the point where they give way and turn into ships themselves.

A small boat, a submarine, a bas-relief of a shipwreck and a low-angle shot of a statue of a sailor. Then the monument to Arturo Prat (1879–1884).

In mid-shot, feet coming down some steps. A one-legged man climbing a stairway. Then a shot of him in close-up. A woman with a kid in her arms comes down a stair wedged between two houses. A little girl coming down on the hand-rail, then a shot of a group of children on their way down behind a dog. Then more shots of stairways. A little girl running with a bunch of flowers in her hand. A vegetable market with stalls set up along some steps. Some kids roll down the slope on carts, while others have fun on the zig-zag steps. An old man hangs on to the rail as he climbs the stairs. He makes his bundle serve as a walking-stick, setting it down at each step. A hen makes its way up the steps.

Up, down, up, up, down, up.
A one-legged man climbs the stairs. 121 steps. He knows how many, he counts them.
You need a stout heart and a good memory too.

The ramp takes you down ten times faster than the steps. You come down ten times faster than you go up.
You laugh as you come down.
You gasp for breath as you go up.

It's funny, it's exhausting, it's ghastly, joyous, inhuman, solemn, ridiculous, strange.

Too many people up there, too few down below: in just an hour it will be the other way round.

A never-ending capture and re-capture like the fortress of Douaumont.
A war-time action or a great manoeuvre, with assaults, sallies, breakthroughs, withdrawals, victories, routs.
And sometimes a truce.

At the top of a hill, in among the hovels, there is a sports field. A whistle blows and we see a football match. The spectators under a coca-cola sign. The goal-keeper misses the ball at one point and we see it rolling down the steps. Two kids positioned further down stop it.

In a narrow street a naval officer goes by followed by his family. A mule slowly climbs a narrow street. On a terrace high above the town some kids send kites flying into the air.

A woman is hanging out her washing on a boat. A stairway, hemmed in by houses on either side, scales the hillside. A wide pan shows the city, the harbour and the harbour buildings. In a narrow street an improvised auction takes place. Fish and sea-food are spread out on the stalls. A mule laden with fish goes by on the quayside.

Close-up of a gull on a rock. We follow the gulls as they wheel and turn in flight, to then re-frame a man taking a dive into the water from a make-shift diving-board. Then another, diving too. A dissolve into the foam shows us a sea-lion having fish thrown to it. Gulls diving and close-up of the seal leaping out of the water to catch the fish. Zoom down onto a fishing-boat where the fishermen are unloading crates of fish which they heap up on carts. A lift-shaft with the cable traction wheel in the foreground. The city is spread out in the distance.

Washing hangs at windows and balconies. A lift goes up and disappears among the unassuming little houses.

You don't starve by the sea. There is fish. But fish don't fly. So it's lifts again. The lifts are very picturesque. But the people who live on the heights depend on them for the necessities of life. And there are some things the lifts can't take up to them. The water they don't have, for instance. And still the washing blows, and the girls wear white blouses. What price those white blouses, those clean faces, when water only comes in cupfuls? What price the most simple things, like washing and cooking? What price the will to live? What price happiness?

Various shots of women, in mid-shot: at the windows of poor houses, on a wooden balcony. A child climbs an old stairway. A woman on her doorstep cossets her baby and another, in the window of a shack, does the same. Women hang washing outside the windows of their hovels. The one-legged man is being led along a road by his wife. At the window of a shanty-town dwelling a young girl is putting curlers in her hair.

An invalid is lowered down a wooden ladder, with extreme care. An old woman seems to be watching as she hangs out her washing at the window. Lifts. We observe the passengers at the ticket office. Sailors, women, young men . . . All with something that has to be taken up: a tyre, a bicycle, flowers, packages, wooden boards, a fish . . .

Everything goes up by way of the lifts. There are some thirty of them. Very few accidents, but they do break-down. Until the lift is repaired the whole life of the hillside is upset. Operators and ticket collectors see the whole town go by; they know its intrigues and its secrets as no-one else does. They are the keepers of the museum of the hills.

Inside the lift-cage the young man with the bicycle has an animated conversation with the young girl, throughout the ascent. The old man smokes his cigarette butt. Another passenger is lost in thought.

The passengers leaving the lift on the terrace at the top. Pan over a maze of iron footbridges where washing is hanging. At the foot of a column a meal is cooking on an open fire. High-angle close-up of a smiling child. Reverse shot of a little girl leaning her elbows on the hand-rail of a stairway. Washing drying all along the walls of the shanty dwellings. A few drops of water drip from a tap into a gutter that acts as a water channel.

The hills have names: the hill of the Baron, the Cross, the Butterfly, the Nuns, the Milkmaids. The higher you climb the poorer people are. At the top the poorest of the poor. Round each hill a belt of big black rusty iron houses. The castles of the poor. How can they live?

The hills are against them. So that a few pennies can be saved the children never use the lift. Water is needed, so is gas, a school, a clinic, drains.

A woman fills a tub with water. We see the backwards and forwards movement of a pulley with a bucket hooked onto it. A man is cranking the pulley forward with a hand-winch. He uses a tin-can to fill the bucket.

Above all, water.

Some have worked out a solution with iron and some rope. But the problem exists for everyone.

A master-shot of a committee as it meets under wooden cross-beams. The three members presiding at the table take out manuscripts and files.

(*Voice-over*) More housing is needed if we are going to put an end to the serious sanitation problems we have in our district, right at the heart of the first port in the country.

Mid-shot of two elderly women.

(*Voice-over*) That was why it was essential to get the public and private builders interested. The Administrator of the province has promised to help us.

Low-angle shot of a man listening, his jacket over his arm. Shot of the front row of the main body of the meeting. A young mother with a child on her knee. Shot of the three presiding at the table. A man in the main body of the meetings puts up his hand and says:

(*The man*) The works committee knows that the builders and the owners aren't in agreement. It's another delay.

A woman in the centre of a group.

(*The woman*) We need water urgently. We're still being rationed and we can't see when it's going to end.

In a dance hall festooned with lights, some young people are dancing to the music of an American record (rock and twist). Various shots of legs, faces, couples dancing, alternating with master-shots of the whole dance floor. A shot of the harbour at night. The lights of the city shimmer around it. A long tracking-shot takes us along an avenue that is a blaze of neon-lit colour. We go back to the dance hall to watch a Chilean dance. Every partner carries a handkerchief which is used to make circular movements in time to the music. Then there is a samba. The camera singles out one of the young girls in the room.
    The alarm is raised that the wooden houses are on fire. The firemen are battling against disaster. One of them coming down a ladder. Someone jumping out of a window. People rushing to look. Firemen using axes to cut down the blazing timbers and prevent the fire from spreading.
    Close-up of an axe as it hacks down a pile of burning wood. The firemen save what furniture they can: an iron bedstead . . .

When there is a fire, it burns with a vengeance. In fact the entire male population belongs to the fire-brigade. Wooden houses, to say nothing of the wind . . .

Close-up of a wooden figurine that acts as a weather-vane on a windowledge. Fish being dried on a line, washing hanging. A child rushing down the hill towards the harbour. People climbing a stairway – one of them carrying a mattress on his back. A man, followed by his dogs, is smiling as he descends an outside spiral staircase. We go back to the man with the mattress as he comes towards us at the top of the hill.

The wind blows hard up there. It's good for drying the washing, not so good for the children's lungs. At least the air is pure and clear. This is the third element of Valparaiso: the air of the hills – in a way like its look.

Like the look of this calm, courteous, rather melancholy people, who are kind to animals and love quiet pleasures: a look that can gladly be returned with the same calmness, courtesy, friendship . . .

Some children are playing in a court yard; squabbling, sliding down the stair-rails. Two others are fencing with sticks. In an alley-way a donkey laden with suitcases, while in the background the man with the mattress climbs on. On a hillside a man and a woman put up a small circus tent that stands out in the midst of the shanty huts. Under the tent the trapeze artist appears in the centre of the ring: he takes a bow. Then a shot of him doing his act. The audience of children shouts, whistles and claps. Then there is a slapstick encounter between two clowns. A 'woman acrobat' does a cartwheel. The man with the mattress walking slowly on the crest of the hill. Two children on a crudely fashioned see-saw in a square. The lifts, and then a pan revealing, alongside, the man with the mattress reaching the top of the very last flight of stairs. He props his mattress against the wall of a house, while close by some children play with a ball.

A man on a horse rides into a horse enclosure on the hill. Shot of a woman beside a quartered carcass hanging in front of a scale.

Around this town of sailors there is a race of horsemen. The butcher's shop on the hill is called 'Buffalo Bill'.

Pan up towards the ceiling where we see a fresco representing three horses sitting drinking at a table. Another represents a race track. Men on a stand looking through binoculars are following a race that goes past the camera, with a low-angle shot of the winning horse. The public behind the tracks. We follow a race. A young woman follows it through binoculars: she seems worried. Another shot of the stands. In mid-shot a galloping horse, whipped by its jockey. Men shouting and gesticulating in one of the stands. Another shot of the fresco: one of the horses with a glass in its hand and a sad expression. Shot of the winning horse posing for a photograph with its owner's arms around its neck.

Near Valparaiso, in Vina del Mar, a horse has won the Grand Prix. It is his moment of glory. Let him make the most of it.

In a narrow street that is perilously steep, a horse carrying a bed. He moves with difficulty and is pushed along by a young man. Riders push the horses into the corrals. They mark a large black cross on each horse's rump. Shot of the horses' heads as they are crowded close together. We go back to the fresco: one horse smoking and laughing, the other one sad.

After five years the horse enters the life of the city: up, down, up, down. But up there *Buffalo Bill's* butcher shop is waiting for its meat.

A black cross on a horse is the sign of death. And the horse blinks its eyes in fear, for it *knows*.

In a field, a low-angle shot of a half-starved horse as he moves in a circle. In mid-shot a knife cuts up a joint of meat. Another shot of the fresco: the horse with a tureen full of playing cards in front of him.

Close-up of a hand laying down cards on a table. We see a fortune-teller. A man opposite her is listening. On a work-bench a model ship on its metal plate. The hands of the fortune-teller picking up the cards. The model maker puts a ship-in-a-bottle on the mantelpiece. Close-up of the bottle. Pan to a fresco of a mermaid.

But men don't *know*. Or they don't want to know. They think of their future as immortal, contained in a tightly closed bottle. At least something of them will remain.

When uneasiness touches them with its cold fingers, instinct leads them towards the warmth and light.

We see a 'sailor's night-club' in a mirror reflection. Couples dancing. Men gambling at a table. 'Girls' on the look-out for business. At one table a man kissing a woman. A girl is drinking at the bar. Another walks past the gambling table and glances at it as she goes by. Close-up of the mermaid on the wall looking at her reflection in a mirror. A sailor sits down on a bench with a girl on either side. Couples dancing. Right beneath the mermaid a woman echoes her gesture as she makes up in front of a hand mirror – immediately beside the men at the gambling table. Close-up of the girl glancing at one of the men. One of the gamblers realizes what they are up to. He drives a dagger into the middle of the table: the fight starts. He throws a glass at the mirror and it breaks. A large red stain appears, spreading on a white background. (From this point on the film is in colour.)

A pack of cards is shuffled in a kaleidoscope. Through the pieces of broken glass we move in on the cards. We are back with the fresco of the mermaid, this time in colour. An old globe of the world is rotating. A skull and crossbones burning. Then we see engravings of pirates and soldiers at arms. A painting of a Spanish general. Two engravings of scenes of torture.

This is the fourth element of Valparaiso: blood.
And its memory.
The memory of pirates: Hawkins, Drake, Joris de Spilbergen. Torture

and pillage.

The memory of the Spanish. Torture and pillage and centuries of colonial oppression.

Engravings of sea battles and battle scenes, an old map of Chile. Close-up of flames. An engraving of Valparaiso in flames. Another of ships in a raging storm. A painting of a desert island with shipwreck survivors desperately signalling for rescue. A rough sea lashing on the rocks.

The memory of fire. The elements are a challenge to man. After fire, the sea.

The memory of storms. Jules Verne's boats cast ashore the shipwrecks of Gavarni.

Close-up of a cannon mouth firing. A portrait of Isabel II. An engraving of the bombardment. The earth opens up and bubbling liquid gushes out. Engravings of earthquakes. Dead fish washed up on the sand.

And so it goes on.

England supports Chile's independence.

Isabel II of Spain has the city bombarded.

The final shudder of the thwarted coloniser.

In its turn the ground opens up. Earthquakes, floods, fires, cyclones and looting. This was to be the fate of this peace-loving people.

And it did not end there.

A cartoon satirising 'Uncle Sam', driving a nail into Panama. A mermaid watches over a ship. A bunch of seaweed, conjuring up streaming hair, floats in the troughs of the waves. Then different statues of mermaids.

But when is there an end? The mermaids in the harbour have not ended their song. They are there, watching, listening, waiting.

Flags being run up at mast-heads. The traffic of the harbour, then back to the shots of the lifts bringing us to the old houses crowded round the lift-shafts. We come back down towards the harbour, where the gulls circle over the docks.

Neither the language of the flags nor the regular rhythm of the ships seem an answer to what once was the adventure of Valparaiso.

But nostalgia for yesterday's adventure is a comfortable escape from today's. With the first good wind on these hills the great kite-flying championship will begin, with its duels, its feints, its triumphs. The adventure is to conquer houses fit to live in, gardens where things will grow, justice.

This is today's adventure. It is another image of adventure. And the grand-children of the builders will perhaps play builders, just as we played pirates.

Paper streamers and kites coiled in the sky. Near the harbour we follow a wedding-party into a church. Gulls swoop down on barges. Children throwing streamers that get caught up in the electricity cables. Then another shot of them as they race downhill to pick up a kite. Then various shots of the championship. As the camera follows them we see the whole city and the port. Shots of a little girl, in mid-shot. Inside a lift the bride's veil streams in the wind. Then a shot of the lift coming down, showing us the city and the port.

Hardi, les gars, vire au gindeau *(Hurrah me bullies, heave the capstan O)*
Good bye, farewell, good bye, farewell
Hardi, les gars, adieu Bordeaux *(Hurrah me bullies, farewell Bordeaux)*
Hourra, of Mexico, ho, ho, ho
Au Cap Horn il ne fera pas chaud *(At Cape Town boys it won't be so hot)*
A faire la pêche au cachalot *(Fishing me boys for big cachalot)*
Haul away, hé, oula tchalez
Hâl' matelot, hé, ho, hisse, hé, ho
Good bye, farewell, good bye, farewell
Adieu misère, adieu bateau *(Goodbye to the drudgery, goodbye to the ship)*
Hourra, oh Mexico, ho, ho, ho
Et nous irons à Valparaiso *(Then we'll be bound for Valparaiso)*
Haul away, hé, oula tchalez
Où d'autres laisseront leurs os *(Where others of us will leave our bones)*
Hé, ho, hisse, hé, ho.

The final credits come up on the right of the screen while on the left we see the shifting images of a kaleidoscope.

(published in *L'Avant-Scène* 1967)

(translated by Liz Heron.)

Joris Ivens: articles and interviews

Some reflections on avant-garde documentaries

Published in *La Revue des Vivants*, no. 10, October 1931, and therefore written with the recent experience of the Filmliga and Ivens' first commissions – *We are Building* and *Philips-Radio* – in mind, this short article resumes some of the theses of that activity. Of particular interest for Ivens' career as a whole are the criticism of the limitations imposed by work in the film industry, the emphasis on the creation of an *active* audience through avant-garde cinema, the need for specifically cinematic means of expression, and the comparison between the independent film-maker and the skilled artisan, with access to his own means of production.

I

The documentary is the expression of reality in its causal and inevitable aspect.

We should note that the documentary is the only means by which avant-garde film-makers can still struggle against the Film Industry. Though not because of the Film Industry in itself, but because the documentary expresses reality as it is, whereas, in general, the Industry produces bad films that pander to the public's bad taste by adapting to it or even drawing inspiration from it, without ever attempting to provoke any activity or reaction from the public.

Avant-garde cinema on the other hand tends to interest spectators and provoke reactions from them.

What I call avant-garde cinema is a cinema which takes the initiative for progress, under the vigilant banner of filmic sincerity. Independent cinema enjoys in fact an auto-critique which helps it along the road of progress, whereas industrial cinema knows only the yardstick of success, that is, the judgment of an ill-educated public.

Industrial cinema only brings technical progress. Avant-garde cinema adds spiritual progress.

II

In the sound film are concentrated all the future possibilities of television and radio. This gives us new reasons for struggling against the tasteless inspiration which constantly threatens the Film Industry.

III

The avant-garde film-maker can find in the documentary a positive way of working; and through the documentary he can give his utmost, as a representative of the expression of the masses and of popular expression in his work.

Because the documentary film must rely mainly on orders, and because it represents the best possible publicity for the industrialists, its maker need only deal with one man: a businessman who is foreign to the cinema. It is therefore in the interest of the film-maker to produce a good film, a film whose only criterion is to be truthful and to possess documentary character.

As against this, when he works for the Film Industry, he must grapple with administrative councils, artists, and censorship. He is limited, he is no longer independent and, so to speak, he finds himself enslaved in some way. To escape from this slavery, he needs to be of great clarity . . . he needs to convince the spectators, whether they belong to an industrial milieu or not.

IV

In the present state of the cinema, the documentary is the best way to discover where the cinema's real path of development lies. It is not possible for the documentary to turn into theatre, literature, music hall – or anything else that is not cinema.

This is a very old thesis, but I should like to repeat myself and recall it, because the sound film is facing today the same dangers that the early cinema faced but gradually managed to avoid.

The cinema is a profession. The independent film-maker is an artisan. He is in possession of an indispensable technique, though not at the expense of spirituality and intellect. That is why there is something to be gained from the Film Industry. A good American cameraman makes a greater contribution to the cinema than a poet; he thinks of himself as a medieval craftsman who can realise on a large scale the idea conceived by the intellectual, thanks to his perfect knowledge of his materials. A good cameraman makes a better film than a poet, because he has better knowledge of the materials and of the technique involved, and this provides him with novel possibilities. I would go as far as to say that when a poet's idea is excellent, it is only by chance, because he does not possess the indispensable cinematic way of thinking.

V

The documentary film-maker cannot lie, cannot fail to be truthful. Matter does not admit of treason: a documentary requires the development of the film-maker's human personality, since the artist's personality is what distinguishes him uniquely from banal actuality, from the mere act of taking pictures.

The good film-maker lives surrounded by matter, by reality. In order to interpret this reality, on each occasion he only chooses one part of it. The success of his film depends both on the confidence the masses have in his

99

personality, and, born from this confidence, on an individual human personality which chooses only the one side of reality that seems important and leaves all else aside.

In other kinds of film there can be no such real and important criterion by which to evaluate the personality of the film-maker.

VI

The documentary must not remain a grounds for emotion or literary excitement at the beauty of matter; it must draw reactions and provoke latent activities.

Because of its excessive individualism and its surfeit of artistic spirit, Europe is resistant to the social action of the documentary.

I therefore believe that I will achieve the development of my idea, of my cinematic ideal, only in Russia, where the masses are being made familiar with these activities, and where they can understand the social truth of the documentary.

(translated by E. G. Noujain)

400 million

100

Collaboration in Documentary

This article, reworked later and incorporated into *The Camera and I*, is the fruit of Ivens' work in America. In it he discusses closely the work of the different members of the film crew, problems with sponsors, non-actors and so on. In 1966, revising the material for *The Camera and I*, he commented: 'I stated, perhaps a little too categorically for someone who started out with nothing more than a wish and a handcamera, that "the day of the one-man documentary is over". What a number of contradictions today collide with this remark! But even though technical and artistic inventions have brought advances and apparatus that once again place total physical control in the hands of a single, solo film-maker, it is still my opinion that any film, including any documentary, has so many sides to its content and its expression that its ideal author is a *team*, a collective of people who understand each other. Such a team is quite different in my mind from a crew formed by a producer who wants to bring certain names and talents together.' (*The Camera and I*, p226)

The day of the one-man documentary film is over. The problems are too manifold and the processes too complex to be handled satisfactorily by a single man. The director still has the responsibility for the film as a whole. The initial conception is most often his, and his constant concern over all the processes will inevitably give the film the colour of his personal style.

Nevertheless, the director works with a group as skilled in their functions as he is in his, and his leadership over them is only temporary. It exists in a realisation of his dependence upon them and of the inter-dependence of the members of his group. An understanding of the relationships within such a group is of vital importance to the *profundity* and *quality* of our documentary films. You make a film not by a belt-system, but by team-work.

In saying that, I do not believe I am talking only for myself. The principles underneath this kind of film we are making seem to dictate this approach. But generalisations alone are not of much use to the young documentary director. I've tried to note below some of my experiences and conclusions. They must in no sense be considered final principles, but merely working notes, to be read in the light of the reader's own experiences. If one person's difficulty is overcome, that will have justified making such a record.

I

There is little opportunity for complete re-evaluations during shooting on location, but there is an important point where a new valuation is inevitable. This is after one of the first days of work on location. Here is the first clash of fact with the early concept written into the script. At this time, one feels that more imagination than knowledge of the real subject has gone into the making of the script. This is naturally more of a disappointment for the young director than an older documentary maker, for he has not yet become hardened to expect this disappointment, which actually should serve as a stimulus to the director.

The director must be extremely sensitive to this clash with reality. In it lie all the several directions (bad as well as good) that his film can take. It is possible to keep the film aloof from the world around it, but this can only do harm to a documentary film – even one that is reconstructing the past. In making documentaries, there can't be four protective walls around your set. Your set is the real world, and you have to look all around you before focussing your camera on a corner of it. Even if you wished to keep aloof, life has a way of making your film a part of it. A documentary film about a war, for example, is very closely connected with the mood of the people fighting that war. In China we found that the concrete day-to-day shifts in the political and military situation affected the course of production. In Spain, the same thing – but in an additional sense, for there the enemy regarded a man with a camera as a distant target no different from anyone else, and was just as eager to blow him and his Eyemo to bits. In our film on farm-life in Ohio, very far from the danger of shrapnel, we began by being deeply involved in the process of film-making, while the farmer was still most concerned with the harvesting of his crop. When we ended, months later, the situation was neatly reversed: the farmer was much more interested in our film, but we were more concerned about the harvesting of his crop.

In general, though, all large mutual re-adjustments between the location and the script should be gotten over with in the first few weeks. Once the director and writer have fixed on the general construction, the line of the shooting should be kept steady – but the details must, and will, continue to be affected by the reality of your subject, place and people. These are facts not usually realised by the layman.

The earliest relationship to be affected by this first contact between concept and reality is the *sponsor*. Before leaving for the location, the director and sponsor have agreed on a script (after the natural struggles of that stage), then in coming to location this earlier concept has had to undergo change. Straightening this out is sometimes difficult because the sponsor is not in contact with the real thing that the director is experiencing.

If yard-long telegrams (that never resolve the disagreement anyway) are to be avoided, the sponsor must have confidence in the director long before he leaves for location, confidence in the director's experience, honesty, knowledge or just prestige. If this trust has not been gained before the film is begun, there is little point in beginning the film.

In the case of a business firm being the sponsor – as in my film for the Philips Electrical Works in Holland – this confidence is as necessary as if the shooting group is a continent away, and not in the factory behind the main offices. In this case, though, the sponsor has a right to point to things in the factory – say a machine waiting for a patent – that must not be photographed. But even this right is limited. A prohibition against taking three men eating a box-lunch should be fought bitterly, because this touches the warm reality that divides an advertising film from a documentary film.

It was in China, unfortunately, that this sort of supervision (not from the sponsor, however) stood between me and reality. Our greatest difficulty was not with a military censorship, which should have full control in war-time, but with a narrow civil censorship of the most human aspects in and behind the front – ordinary crowds of people, single faces, ordinary streets and landscapes. The fiction films usually made about China have certainly justified their care in this matter, but I regret this loss every time I see the completed *400,000,000*.

Often a fundamental disagreement with the sponsor never occurs. The most obvious example of such a situation is when the film-maker is part of the sponsoring body, as in History Today, the producer of *400,000,000*. There are other cases where this is also true. In making *Borinage,* the sponsor was the Belgian Mine Workers Union – constantly pushing Storck and myself deeper into the material, asking us to give more reality, since the aim of the film was to better bad conditions. And how faithfully we answered this demand of the sponsor can be judged from the French censor's phrase in banning *Borinage* – *'trop de réalité'!* * [. . .]

A typical crew working continuously on location on a documentary film should include: director, writer, cameraman, assistant cameraman, and business manager. If necessary, and where the budget is severely limited, some of these functions can be held by one person. For example, the director might also be the writer, or the writer might take on the job of assistant cameraman.

Inevitably, this group of four or five people, even if they are not ordinarily difficult, are somewhat different when they are away on location or on an expedition. They are separated from their friends and wives and ordinary habits. Therefore the director has not only to be an artist, the creative source of the film, and an engineer who can superintend all the various techniques, but he must be a group-leader as well. These four or five people are all necessary and important in the practice of an art, and the director as 'group-leader' has to realise that in documentary films there is the realistic possibility of every group member (particularly the cameraman) moving up into direction soon. Thus he has the responsibility of developing the directive abilities of the group.

The *writer* of a documentary film can be chosen for any one of a wide variety of reasons, but there is one very important factor: that is whether he will be able to accompany the crew on to location. This procedure has been

*'Too much reality!'

103

repeatedly proven to me of such value that I now consider it a necessity, where the film has an elaborate theme. It is a test of the writer's view-point and his imagination, and is of the utmost importance to the progress of the film. Shaping the constant change of reality into the dramatic structure of the growing work, and becoming interested and involved in social, political and even seasonal changes in the environment – on a documentary film the writer's work is never done till the film is done.

The writer can be a big help in the director's responsibilities to the group, by helping him with the conferences that keep them in touch with the changing situation, on location, with the home office and with the rest of the world. With the director and cameraman usually dog-tired at the end of the day, prevented from thinking creatively, the writer is depended upon to be their spur, to broaden the film's subject, in drama and in detail, while they are all away from the specificity of the camera. Another, and rather particular way in which the writer, with his relatively greater leisure at this time, can help the director, is to become aware of each member of the group as a person, sensing needs and troubles before they are expressed. He must help to keep the group happy, a point which will be understood by anyone who has suffered in doing film work in a glum atmosphere, which only gets glummer while it is neglected.

On the other hand, the writer is subject to certain difficulties by his very presence on location. A special danger, at the time of the first clashes between the concept and reality, is the temptation to cast aside his literary qualities, relying entirely on the strong visuals around him. This has to be guarded against by the director.

Outside influences affect the *cameraman* too, and the director and writer must protect him from everything that makes his job any more physically exhausting than it already is, even to carrying the camera. The cameraman should have an *assistant*, if at all possible, to keep the work moving quietly – and to relieve him of a quantity of technical detail that would otherwise make a hard job harder.

Whether the cameraman has been hired for one film or he is a team-mate who has grown up with you – you, as the director, must know his job well enough to help him daily with all his camera and light problems – a directorial function that would be unthinkable in Hollywood. It hardly seems necessary to point out that he should be ready for any emergency, favourable or not, and a sense of humour is very helpful. He should, of course, have a special feeling for this particular film form.

And finally, the first day's work will be the crucial test of your *business manager*. If it ran smoothly, it's to his credit. He is also the group economist and the group absorber of all prop and money problems.

II

[. . .] On the whole, we all recognise the danger of too much naturalism in our documentary work. We are learning to conceive documentary film as an emotional presentation of facts. Therefore we must learn to think of a documentary as requiring a wide variety of styles – all for the purpose of achieving the maximum expressiveness and conviction.

If a kitchen is to be made more memorable, to be made an epitome of all the kitchens in that neighbourhood – you must make many adjustments and re-arrangements, not for aesthetic reasons alone, but to heighten the content value of that scene. On the other hand, in making adjustments of this sort, one must be careful not to spoil the spontaneity of living places, or manufacture an artificially harmonious surrounding. Perfection can often kill spontaneity.

In filming *Borinage* there were instances when the objects in front of the camera were too satisfying aesthetically; sometimes the poverty and dirt had tonal values that caught the eye pleasingly. Our job was to prevent the audience from being distracted away from unpleasant facts by agreeable objects. As in music, there is often a need for dissonance in saying (or yelling) what you want your audience to hear. The cameraman must be made aware of your basic purpose behind such directives, both as respects objects and people [. . .]

Once upon a time most of us were interested in photographing gadgets and when we photographed the movements of people, they looked like gadgets too. You can see it in many passages in my *Industrial Symphony*. Now I try to reveal the human being's relation to the objects around him – and to each other. [. . .]

I advise not to fool with a man's professional pride. Don't ask a farmer to milk an empty cow, even though it's just for a close-up of the farmer's face. He fights such an idea because to him it is false – until he has been with the filming group for a long time.

Even as simple a rule as 'Don't look at the camera' is bound up with the man himself. But this is such a basic necessity for the quality of your film that you must enforce the rule even though it hurts you to. I find an instance of this in my Chinese diary, at the time of the battle of Taierchwang:

'April 13, 1938.

'The ambulance corps does not have enough stretcher bearers so that the peasants of the villages work in relays, taking the wounded from their village to the next, where those peasants in turn take them, and and so for miles and miles. The base hospital is far, and there are no roads. We film this.

'I asked Dick (the Chinese interpreter) to try to have the bearers and the wounded not look too obviously at the camera. He doesn't respond as he usually does, and the directions he gives are too vague. I see that the picture will not give the audience the feeling of naturalness, so I ask him to be more to the point with them. He refuses and runs away, and we continue the picture as best we can, and I use the only three Chinese words I know. Good thing I learned them. Boo yao kaan: Don't look this way. It works, but a little mechanically.

'Later, on the way home, I have a long talk with Dick. In a way he is right. He says, "I couldn't yell at my own people, they fought so hard, got badly wounded. I have too much respect for them and therefore I am silent. Directing them not to look would be cruel; I would like to help them." There we are! Of course, *we* also. But our way is to make a good film, to move people by its high professional quality. Then they will feel and understand that the wounded soldier needs a good stretcher for his very life. John (*John Ferno*) and Capa and I have the same respect as Dick but we cannot allow it to influence us when we are doing our work. Of course, objectively, it seems indiscreet and shameless to go so deep into sorrow and private life and emotions, but we learned in Spain and in working with poverty-striken coal miners of Belgium that you have to do this. It is difficult, I can understand Dick. After filming scenes of wounded soldiers, of terrible things in the villages you are more deeply moved than ever, and the feeling of indignation against the Japanese military setup responsible for this becomes even stronger, and with that the will to do something about it. That is part of the tension which you get back many months later in the cutting room in New York, alone with all the film material, when you shape it into an artistic form which will make clear what you have to say to everyone in the audience.

'Dick begins to feel that we were not so cruel as he thought. In the evening we play poker with him and the Generals at the field headquarters. I would ten times rather talk to the sentinel at the gate and with the wounded soldiers this afternoon. It would have been better for the work. The courtesy of the Generals is suffocating and gets on my nerves. So I stop playing poker and I talk with John about the script . . .'

III

Back in the cutting room there is a new set of problems and several new collaborators.

When the rushes are ready, the first problem is often the sponsor again. Unless he has worked very close to the film up till this point or unless he is perfectly familiar with the entire process of the creation of a film, seeing the rushes will do harm – particularly if the sponsor is not an individual, but a group of people with as many different approaches. The rushes usually frighten them. They each think of ten things that should have been shot. They cannot realise the importance of the cutting and sound and music that will complete the film. They will fight among themselves about the factors that concern each of them personally. It is as if all the department heads of General Motors were to be consulted on a colour for the office walls.

The rushes plus the original script can give an excellent idea of the film as it will appear when finished – but only to an experienced film professional. The sponsor's confidence in the director is subjected to a very hard test at this point. My recommendation is to make a specially prepared cutting of the rushes for the sponsoring committee, anticipating its degree of interest and information.

When the rushes are fully cut, and the commentary and music can be indicated roughly, then the sponsor *might* be invited to see the film he has sponsored, but anything before this time is a risk.

The *editor* is one of the new working group. His work with the director (unless the director prefers to do all the silent cutting himself) requires as much team work as the director and cameraman in the field. Although the first job of the editor on a documentary film is to follow the director's directives, the editing process is not merely technical work – it is as creative as the function of the cameraman or composer on the documentary film. Here the editor must have a surer feeling for rhythm than an editor in Hollywood, because the quality of the documentary film cannot depend on a star or other artificial supports for holding an audience's interest.

I'd like to suggest another function for the editor while the crew is still on location. If the director in the field could know that there is one person personally supervising the group's laboratory work, arranging and shipping the rushes, it would mean a lot to his peace of mind (especially since we are not big enough customers to command the lab's individual attention). This person might easily be the editor, working perhaps for two or three groups at a time. Such work, plus his cutting after the group's return, would keep an editor busy the year round, rather than the four working months of the year that an editor now has.

If there are any weaknesses in the material, the director must confess all to the editor, who is the only one who can help to correct any basic faults. Secrets kept from the editor are a risk to the solidity of the finished film.

Contrary to the practice I recommend with the sponsor, I believe all the rushes should be shown to the *composer* before the cutting has actually begun. To see the material at this time gives him a broad idea of it and also gets him started on the key musical ideas. He will see a journey, a sand-storm, a battle, a pastoral episode that will certainly need music. And while the director and editor are bringing the uncut material into clearer shape, the composer is roughing out his thematic material.

But the silent cutting has to be complete before the composer can be asked to actually write the music for the film, although small adjustments have to be made by both director and composer after the writing and before the recording. Even after the recording, there are possibilities for further accenting of the music by shifting shots during the sound cutting. Although it may seem heresy in the music departments of Hollywood for me to say so, I believe that the composer can be a great help with suggestions for the cutting and timing of the visuals.

The *writer of the commentary* (not necessarily the author of the film) has to work in this same period, and with much the same method. He had best keep his nose close to the movieola, and derive his ideas as much from the

107

film as from the script. If he has time, he ought to test and retest his commentary at the screenings, with fullest consciousness of the film's movement as related to his words.

The composer must know the content and emphasis of the commentary, and before final preparations for recording are made, the director, editor, composer, and writer should be familiar with a complete log of the plan for picture, music, commentary and sound.

The conceptions of the sound should have been already developed on location, so that the photography could be calculated with sound in mind. For example, in the barn scene of the film, the sound of the first milk hitting the bucket was a particularly expressive sound that had to be noted for later recording, because it is possible to allow for sound in the photography – filming long enough pan shots to allow the sound to grow, as well as close-ups.

And so finally, you take your precious silent reels to be recorded. The director's relation to the *sound engineer* up to now has not been entirely satisfactory. The director lives with his group on location for many weeks at least, but he is with the sound engineer only for a few hours.

The sound engineer of the present (but not of the future) is pretty solely interested in his mechanics, and doesn't object to being characterised by a lack of imagination and a refusal to take imaginative chances. The development of a new generation of sound engineers is beginning to take place, in spite of the considerable expense of sound experiment. But we must remember that once we were all told that films were too expensive to experiment with. Sound experiment and new sound engineers must receive the same encouragement that films are benefiting from in many philanthropic foundations.

IV

You eventually bring your finished film to the collaborator who has exerted a constant moral pressure upon every function of its making from the start – the *audience*. Our initial mistake, which we are well out of by this time, was placing our documentary work in an avant-garde category of film-making. As soon as we recovered the social function of documentary, we recovered a healthy relation to our audience. This relation requires a study alone, but within this outline of documentary collaboration there are some relevant remarks to be made.

It may be inconsiderate of me to say so, but I believe that the documentary film-maker has a greater responsibility to his audience than the creator of any other kind of films. The very absence of a fictional coating is almost enough cause for this greater responsibility, but add to this that we are constantly touching unfamiliar concepts, social and political themes that the moral propagandists in Hollywood rarely touch, and to influence people's opinions on these closer, but more unusual subjects is a considerable task.

108

Part of the audience already recognises the world and the form of the documentary film, but it is still strange for the majority of the audience. They are as unaccustomed to this 'new' form as a reader of newspapers and novels would be in encountering his first short story.

Any film audience is usually tired before they enter a film theatre. The commercial film realises this and has perfected a technique to keep their audience dreaming awake. Till now the problem of finding our equivalent to this technique remains a series of unsolved questions in my mind. Can you educate a tired audience? How long can a film spectator look at a real person or a real place on the screen without wishing for change or imagination? How much of a fictional treatment can reality bear? Etc., etc.

The answers to such questions can never be wholly theoretical. The director should constantly see films with audiences – his films and others', taking the members of his collective group with him. He must listen, look, and take notes – not of the film, but of the audience.

There is one other relationship I should like to mention before completing this outline, and that is the director's relation to other documentary film-makers and other groups, including the film-critics. We must make up for the lack of grandeur and money by giving special attention to cooperation and advice among ourselves. After too long a period of separate and self-sufficient groups in the field of documentary films in America, we have an opportunity now, in the Association of Documentary Film Producers, to work *together,* no matter how many different films we may be working on as individuals. It is another, and higher, form of collaboration in the documentary.

Long live cinéma-vérité!

Published in *Les Lettres Françaises,* in March 1963, this article comes out of an intervention by Joris Ivens at a conference organised in Lyons to debate and discuss the new possibilities opened up by technical developments in film equipment and the name their users coined to describe their cinematic form – *cinéma-vérité.* Ivens was slow to adopt the new aesthetic, although he used the new lightweight equipment in *Rotterdam Europoort.* In fact, he never became a subscriber to the cult of authenticity. In this article he spells out the reasons for his reserve, although he welcomes the technical achievement. The text by Brecht referred to reads in part as follows:

Those who these days want to fight against lies and ignorance and want to write the truth must overcome at least five difficulties. They must have the *courage* to write the truth despite it being suppressed on all sides; the *intelligence* to distinguish it, even though it is concealed on all sides; the *artistry* to make it manageable as a weapon; the *discrimination* to choose those in whose hands it is effective; the *cunning* to propagate it among them. (Bertolt Brecht, 'Five difficulties faced when writing the truth', 1935).

When a new movement of film art decides to call itself 'cinéma-vérité', it is certainly choosing a very strong term, a term that has considerable meaning for everyone. The choice of the term thus means that we cannot just confine ourselves to examining questions of technique (the technique, besides, could very easily be used to tell lies); it forces us to consider and discuss the artistic and moral aspects of our art.

Some will no doubt wonder whether the choice of term is a happy one, whether the expression 'cinéma-vérité' can really cover all the different types of films that are supposed to go by that name. Originally, the expression was in fact an ill-understood translation of 'Kino-Pravda', the title of a newsreel series by Dziga Vertov. Subsequently, and in order to introduce their films to the wide public, it was used with reference to the work of Jean Rouch, Mario Ruspoli and Richard Leacock. Today the term has become quite popular, and it could not be got rid of easily. Perhaps alternative terms like 'Direct Cinema', 'Sincerity Cinema', 'Spontaneous Cinema', 'Information Cinema' are more modest, but I feel they are not as demanding or as adequate.

An expression like 'cinéma vérité' really forces us to tell the truth. It could become the watchword of the struggle, for there are times when, in some circumstances, it is not always easy to tell the truth.

Perhaps it does not matter what one says in a discussion about this or that label, so long as one makes good films; perhaps these generalisations bring to the discussion nothing but demagogy. Nevertheless, when tomorrow we go back to our cameras it will still be the truth that ought to count . . .

We will then be faced with a host of questions: Which truth and for whom? Seen by whom, and for whom? Will it be the whole truth or only a part of it? In this case, which part? Lastly, to what use will this truth be put?

In 1951 the Pleyel cinema in Paris advertised my films with a poster that said: 'The cinema, weapon of truth'. Nevertheless, there is a kind of truth that does no more than skim the surface of events.

How did the cinema express the truth before the birth of cinéma-vérité?

Ever since the birth of the art of the cinema, to tell the truth has been the aim and the concern of many film-makers. I knew personally both Dziga Vertov and Flaherty, the two precursors of cinéma-vérité. Between us grew a friendship as well as a professional association, and discussions on our work and our projects often revolved around questions like these: What must be the artistic expression of truth, the truth of life in front of our camera? the truth as an expression of ourselves?

It is in the documentary that the direct confrontation of truth with everyday life and reality, that the question of expressing, or rather, of searching for the truth becomes most evident. This to a much greater extent than in feature films, as can be seen from documentaries the world over.

As far as technique is concerned, we have always looked for equipment that was lighter and less noisy. However, as documentary film-makers, we have always encountered difficulties other than the merely technical, namely the problem of penetrating reality more deeply in order to discover in it the expressions of life: the living truth. We have sought technical means that would not affect the natural behaviour of people in front of our microphones and cameras. It is not merely our honesty, but also the technical quality of our films that has become an important factor in resolving the problem, in making the public accept the truth, our own truth.

During the Lyon meeting, we saw the remarkable achievements brought about by the joint efforts of French technicians and film-makers, in particular M. Coutant's camera. The Coutant-Mathot-Eclair is a real camera-eye. It makes the old dream of all documentary film-makers come true. The possibilities it opens up in terms of sound and visuals will not only go to improve technique and form, but they will also reach the content and the fundamental aspects of our work. I would also like to join Georges Rouquier in his hope that the builders of the camera-eye will remember that film-makers, like cosmonauts, would always want to use more and more miniature equipment in order to communicate the great discoveries of modern technology, like the preparations for joint space travel to Mars, Venus or the moon.

The new cameras sit on the cameraman's shoulder like the falcon perched on the falconer's shoulder in the Middle Ages. They are not a mechanical, heavy, noisy, rigid piece of equipment any longer. And the n.icrophone can from now on wander around and listen, like an inquisitive ear. Thus the cameraman can, with his camera, go straight to the heart of the action. For years now I have been telling young film-makers: your camera must be part of the action. But what used to be a vague recommendation has become today a concrete possibility, thanks to the camera-eye.

Having said this, we should remain alert to the fact that with the possibility of quick observation and increased mobility comes the danger of remaining on the surface of truth, of skimming reality instead of penetrating it, of showing it without any force, daring or creative power.

We need to be aware of the dangers that might make us lose along the road the truth we had first set out to express. It is important at the outset to look intensely for the truth in order to express it by an elaborate documentation and an intelligent analysis – for the real truth is often hidden.

The directing of a film, like its conception, will often give rise to moral problems. Richard Leacock said it very clearly in his contribution, and I agree with him: sincerity, honesty, conviction are important elements if we are to fulfil our responsibilities *vis-à-vis* the public; together, these forces give us a better chance of never deviating from the path of the truth.

Many traps might appear in the course of shooting a film: for instance, the overall truth and the authenticity of details might become confused. This is the kind of authenticity which is enormously increased by cinéma-vérité. Another trap is to remain at a static conception of the truth, without becoming aware that by actively following the events and the characters, the aspects of the truth might change. And truth is also at risk at the editing stage, when it becomes easy to lie, consciously or unconsciously.

In some cases, in order to express oneself in cinéma-vérité, one is forced to make militant films. Here some brutal forces may intervene in order to stifle truth in its various forms. I am not here only referring to the censorship of completed films, but to active interventions in the course of shooting. Not long ago, in the course of shooting a film, the Belgian police destroyed the truth (or rather a latent image of it) contained in a film about a dockers' strike in Anvers, by opening the canisters and exposing the film to light.

I have also in mind another film – quite old now – which was shot using the methods of cinéma-vérité. This short film showed that a so-called police operation was in reality a fully-fledged colonial war. It earned its maker eight years of exile. Nor should we forget certain retaliatory methods, like the blacklists aimed at film-makers who dared to tell the truth about their own country.

At a time when it is not everywhere easy to tell the truth, it is both enlightening and comforting to read again the advice given by B. Brecht in an article called, I think, 'Five difficulties in telling the truth'.

In order to talk of cinéma-vérité in the basic sense of the word, we need freedom of expression not only in our cinemas, but also on television.

Our cameras have now become light, mobile, fast and silent. But despite this marvellous tool, truth would continually elude us if we did not have the means to express ourselves freely on the screen, if we would not share our experience, our search for the truth, with the public.

I wish to tell the film-makers of cinéma-vérité that documentary film-makers are on their side, and that many have joined ranks with them. Let them not forget that we are all engaged together on the same arduous road of CINEMA and TRUTH.

(translated by E. G. Noujain)

Interview with Joris Ivens in *Image et Son*, May 1964

This interview, published in a special issue of *Image et Son* dedicated to the use of 16mm, provides a useful view of Ivens the teacher. By 1964 he had taught in many different countries – Poland, China, Chile, the United States among them. Of particular interest are his comments on the role of the commentary and the relationship sound: image.

Q: What, according to you, are the conditions for a really independent cinema, valid in 1930 as well as in 1963?
A: An independent cinema is always the work of small crews. Furthermore, it has always been difficult to find organisations broad-minded enough to support it. For instance, although *Symphonie Industrielle* was commissioned by a large factory, it is still an independent film, because the organisers said to us: 'Look at our factory, you are free, film it as you see it'. This is very valuable, because orders are in general very restricting, placing the artist within too narrow limits. So a commissioned film can still be an independent expression, like A. Resnais' film on styrene. A film-maker must always struggle for his independence, not only for his own sake, but also for the sake of the organisation that employs him, because the best possible propaganda is in fact the work of art.

Q: So, for you, an independent mind is the best guarantee for an independent cinema?
A: Quite, but sometimes it has to be paid for very dearly. You need the guts to say no to some work, but at other times you are forced to accept, in order to make a living. In this case, you should do your work as honestly as possible, but get back to independent cinema at the first opportunity. All this indicates that it is unfortunately not always very easy to make an independent film. Sometimes you need to accept work if only not to lose touch; if so, do your job honestly, but never stop struggling to impose the subject you really care for. You should never give up: nothing might happen the first year, but in the second or third year – or it may even be longer – a friend might come along and help, and one day you'll eventually make your film. So never give up too soon. It is not enough to have a good mind, you also need the will to do it, like an inventor. On this level, organisations like *Image et Son* can be of great help to those who have shown they are determined to make a film. And you can't hope to work alone: if you do, you'll soon end up like Don Quixote in front of his windmills.

Q: In this connection, do you think trade union organisations have done all they could?
A: Not really. Unfortunately, the trade unions seem only interested in the printed word. They do not realise that there are more effective channels to express their demands, now that young people are educated by audio-visual methods and by television. These important media are now only channelling entertainment, and I don't understand why they are being overlooked when it comes to carrying out the struggle, making statements and putting forward demands. There are exceptions, however, as in the case of *Song of the Rivers* which I was commissioned to make by the World Federation of Trade Unions (*Fédération Syndicale Mondiale*). Of course, this is a politically committed film, but to me an independent artist is not someone who abandons his ideology and political convictions.

113

Q: *So, irrespective of whether the order for a film comes from an industrial organisation or a political organisation, the film will still be independent so long as the artist remains sincere but firm?*
A: Yes. Sometimes I am told: 'You say you are independent, but you are politically committed'. Of course I am committed, but on what side? On the side of what I believe, of my convictions, my philosophy and ideology. And this is the way it should be, because every artist is committed. Take medieval painters, for example: they were just as committed as Picasso or Chagall were. Chagall, for instance, is a visionary who can announce events whilst retracing the history of the world. When the fascist menace drew close, red angels started falling from the heavens. So, you see, Chagall is committed, every artist is committed. In *Spanish Earth*, for instance, it is clear that both Hemingway and myself are on the side of the Spanish republicans, on the side of the struggle for democracy. In spite of this, I would maintain that we were absolutely free and independent. Independence is not false objectivity. How, in a time of war, can one make a film which would not be on one side or the other? At any rate, for me, a film that sat on the fence would not even be a work of art, because a work of art must take sides, if only in the broad sense of the term.

Q: *But an independent film-maker cannot tackle everything, because he lacks the means to do so. In your opinion, what areas are particularly suitable for him?*
A: I think for a professional any film can be independent.

Q: *There are, however, a certain number of subjects which can attract producers very easily, and there is hardly any point in making independent films about them. One must therefore tackle those subjects which, for a variety of reasons, may not attract a producer. Isn't it here that we should find the independent cinema?*
A: I can only talk about a particular genre of course: the documentary. And even then, there are different styles for documentaries: lyrical, satirical, didactic, or reportage style. In this sphere there are enormous possibilities. But an independent film-maker could also work in animation, or in short features. There were films of this kind in Evreux. They were interesting, though not always very successful. Independent film-makers must, however, find a style of their own, and in this respect amateurs in particular have an important contribution to make. As far as the professional is concerned, to be independent is very, very difficult. But now that film equipment has been improved, and cinematic culture is more widespread, amateurs are better equipped than they were ten years ago. Technique is today easier, emulsions more sensitive and sound much easier to use. All this means we can expect a lot from amateurs, and that is why I readily accepted going to Evreux. I wanted to see for myself what the situation is and find out about the possibilities of this kind of independent cinema – of which, until then, I knew very little. Now I am really convinced that the renaissance of

independent cinema will come through amateur film-makers. It is true that for the moment we have not had real results, but there is every reason to be hopeful, and I am optimistic. Perhaps the films were not a success, but we certainly saw people who were searching very hard – and that, by itself, is quite a lot.

Q: What do you think of acted films made in the same conditions?
A: I believe they should be cultivated, but only with the greatest care, because they can easily lead to the worst kind of dilettantism, exactly as with amateur theatre. Here, I think amateurs must be very modest, they should not start with the most complicated. Psychological drama is very difficult to make and here the amateur might appear inferior to the professional. It is extremely important to find one's own style, and I had the same problem when I started. One day, a businessman discovers that there is a new style around, and that's a new step forward.

Q: What advice would you give to someone wanting to make documentaries?
A: First of all, try to gain in-depth knowledge of the technique. Then find a theme which is close to you, and which is accessible. Thirdly, you must be enthusiastic about this theme, almost obsessed by it. You should feel miserable if you can't make your film. The amateur must feel that the film he intends to make is of great importance to him. If it is just a matter of saying to oneself one day, 'Well, maybe I'll make a film tomorrow', then it is almost certain to be a bad film. A good film is hard to make, and it requires a lot of work. And, anyway, with any genre, one needs to see other films, to have a cinematic culture, not in order to imitate, but to become aware of the level you must reach.

Furthermore, the most important thing for the young film-maker is to find the money for his film. A grant, a subsidy, some kind of help; or there may be someone directly or indirectly interested by his film. He must also practice, making films even in very bad conditions. Apart from exercise value, this will mean that he will have something to show, and one can sometimes detect a talent that will develop even in what looks like a failed attempt. And it is very important that the young film-maker is helped by others: cine-clubs for instance should organise evening classes, training courses and contacts with professionals.

Q: What do you think of commentaries in amateur documentaries?
A: This is a chronic disease. The role of the commentary is to give, in conjunction with the image, the real aspect of the film's subject. The commentary must participate in the dramatic construction of the film, it must not function merely as an explanation. In a word, it must be *part* of the film. At times, the commentary might begin something which the image will then continue – the image will here be speaking by itself. Or, at other times, the image might start an idea which is then taken up in more depth by

the commentary. In any case, we are here talking about the most difficult problem for young film-makers. Their starting point must be visual, not musical or literary; and the commentary 'disease' often starts in the very conception of the film. Once the images are there, it is easier to find the appropriate commentary. Nowadays, with direct sound, it is often possible to avoid having a commentary: the people themselves speak. If the film-maker does not himself write his commentary, he must ask a writer, and that's a very difficult thing for a writer – though it is not as difficult for a poet. The writer often tries to suggest images with the help of words, and, in a film, what is needed is to find an accompaniment to the images. In the last stages of editing and adding sound to the film, five elements are of great importance: the images, the music, the commentary, the dialogue and the sound effects. These five elements must be tightly related. If the commentary pits itself against the image by talking too much and trying to be autonomous, it will ruin the image, even if the image is excellent. Giving each element the same tone is also to be avoided: if an image is lyrical, and the music and the commentary are lyrical too, that's very bad, because they will all contradict each other. By using a dry music and a news-style commentary with a very lyrical image, you achieve a much more lyrical whole than if the commentary tried to have the same effect as the image. That's something I am always telling young people: you must measure the elements of a film very carefully in order to come up with a well-balanced whole. The same applies to the music. It is important to know at what point the spectator will feel the need to hear it, and it must not be to the detriment of the image. Every young film-maker should use as an example a film which he feels is very good, and he must analyse this film in detail on a viewing table. He will soon find that effects are achieved by split-second timing: a particular note must be heard on this or that image, otherwise the whole effect is lost. This is the kind of timing which makes a film like *Muriel* so important: a note or two used by Resnais at a most precise moment. Sometimes, I try to use the commentary like a springboard: at the beginning of one scene, so as to help me steer the spectators towards the best way of interpreting the following scene. I then leave the spectators absolutely free to see and think for themselves. At the end of a scene, I might use the commentary again so as to say, as it were, 'You were right in thinking that, but here's an aspect that you might have missed'. When used in this way, the commentary stands at the hinges of the film. Films are often boring because spectators do not need to think, because everything is thought out for them by the commentary. Spectators must always be invited to think, and if the commentary is too obvious, it will put them to sleep. A commentary that chokes itself, says everything, explains everything, will soon make its public passive, sleepy, and certainly uninterested. Another thing: the commentary must be spoken by a pleasant, well-chosen voice. It must not attempt to impose itself from the very start: let the images begin, the commentary will follow. The commentary should be a friend by the spectator's side, helping him and guiding him, but without being pretentious. Take for example *Song of the Rivers*: for a full minute, the film opens up with a succession of very beautiful images. Then, echoing the spectator's own thought, the commentary says: 'Yes, nature is beautiful . . .' At this point a complicity is established and the commentary can go on to say '. . . but it too is the work of man'. And so the public is prepared to listen. I also like the commentary to change tone throughout the film, sometimes being dry, sometimes gentle, satirical, etc . . .

(translated by E.G. Noujain)

Interview with Joris Ivens in *Filmfaust*, December 1976

On October 11/12, 1976, Alexandra Kluge and Bion Steinborn from the German magazine *Filmfaust* conducted a long interview with Joris Ivens and Marceline Loridan in Paris. The following extracts are from the interview with Joris Ivens published in *Filmfaust* vol. 1. nos. 1–2. In these extracts Ivens talks about his political philosophy, the significance of documentary *vis-à-vis* fiction forms, and reflects on their meaning for his own film practice, developed over fifty years of film-making.

Q: All your life you have been close to people in struggle often in extremely dangerous situations. Would you lead such a life if you were starting again?
A: Certainly I would take the same path. It wouldn't be exactly the same, because you do nothing a second time without seeing more, understanding more and deepening your experience. But it is important to take a path with the same loyalty to the idea of revolution. It is the only path for me. One should never present such decisions as a sacrifice – as sometimes happens. I want to take just that path and no other – and I therefore accept all its consequences. Your question exaggerates a little when you say that I have often put my life in danger. I have often been with men who have put their lives into danger, but that is not the most important thing. When Marceline Loridan and I were shooting a film like *The Seventeenth Parallel*, we were exposed for three months to the same danger as the population. Three months with US bombing from three sides. But after three months we put our film cans under our arms and went to do the editing somewhere else, at an editing table. There were no bombs there, only occasional explosions of feeling. So you shouldn't exaggerate the danger under which a revolutionary film-maker lives. You should always look at this danger in comparison with the people who are involved, with the person involved in it whom you have filmed – in comparison with the risks they run, ours is minimal. Because for a people in revolution the risk of death is as great before you film as after. If you wanted to compare the path taken by a revolutionary film-maker with the Long March of the Chinese revolutionaries, I could

only say 'I marched a tiny bit of the road with them' [. . .]

I am sure that it is revolutionary to put your camera at the service of liberation. But that is not enough. After my hands and feet I have to put my head as well at the service of liberation, so that the whole of me is used, with all its rich possibilities, in liberation from oppression, from exploitation and humiliation. I must approach things with the method of 'dialectical materialism' and analyse the contradictions of world history etc. in that way – and never lose sight of the revolution.

I am neither a realist nor a prophet, and therefore when I was in China in 1938 I could not foresee that the Chinese revolution would win so quickly. But one result of the marxist-leninist method of research was that when I was there at that time I came across many of the latent revolutionary forces and I saw many young people going north to Yenan, to join in the fight with Mao Tse-Tung, Chu-Teh and Chou-en-Lai for the liberation of China. And I saw the Red Army growing in size and fighting. I saw how the revolutionary forces within the Chinese people were growing stronger and stronger. And that gave me the courage to think that the Chinese revolutionaries would surely win, because they visibly put themselves at the service of the Chinese people and demonstrated that they were convinced that they could bring them independence and freedom. I believe that a documentary film-maker and a revolutionary film-maker should start, as I have done all my life, from the heated moments of history, and make films which are not just reportage. Films which are not attached at any price to so-called reportage, but which attempt immediately to try to uncover a deeper reality. I mean, you shouldn't illustrate the superficial authenticity of events, you must go deeper and that means really coming to terms with people. If you want to win the confidence of people in struggle you have to tell them why you are making the film. Who you want to address. And they will want to discuss with you what they can do about that. You must always try to establish a relationship of equality in front of and behind the camera. I'm saying nothing that I haven't already said: a documentary film-maker and a revolutionary film-maker must really come to terms with people if he really wants to make a film with them. But confidence alone isn't enough. Each must also be ready to learn from the other. Without that, you can't make a film. It is even better if this mutual apprenticeship takes place in a conscious way and both sides want it from the beginning. But it is necessary. Every time you find yourself in a new situation you have to be a bit modest. You must not think and behave as if you already know everything, just because you think and are certain that you possess the correct ideology and the necessary enthusiasm. That isn't enough.

Q: We are asking you these questions not just because the route you have taken seems to us exemplary, but also because we are perplexed that only a small number of the representatives of the French avant-garde and the new German cinema, who mostly say they are on the left and sometimes that they are revolutionaries, treat you as a member of the avant-garde who struggles for socialist films and liberated cinema. But there are certainly good reasons for that and we can discuss them later on. In the meantime we would like to have your opinion on the characteristics of the documentary film as compared with the fiction film. You have tackled this question before.

A: You want to know why, in France and in Germany, none of the younger generation of film-makers has taken my work as an example, or followed the same path?

Q: Yes. Their roots are almost exclusively bourgeois – René Clair, Max Ophuls, Alfred Hitchcock, Fritz Lang. Only one of them refers at all to the marvellous revolutionary Soviet film-makers – Eisenstein, Vertov, Pudovkin, Dovzhenko. And the Ivens tradition, which is still alive, is ignored. Is this because you are a revolutionary film-maker, or because you are the only revolutionary still alive, who is still making the history of socialist cinema, which these people do not want?

A: You need someone better than me to answer your question, don't you? Personally, I have never thought of my work as exemplary. I believe that everyone has their own example – others give an example, not you yourself. I believe that it depends on the political situation whether young film-makers at a particular moment have the desire to make films like mine – militant or combative films. Unfortunately they don't always have the necessary patience. Everything has to happen quickly – success, in the first place, which isn't so important if it is the bourgeoisie which is bringing the house down. But I believe that above all they don't see how to link their cinematic practice to their ideology. The two are completely dissociated. It is most important to establish this link, and this is the condition of making a revolutionary film. Without establishing this very strict relationship between theory and practice, without an incessant struggle with contradictions to push towards a new unity, everything you do remains dead and abstract and works to the advantage of the dominant power. And when you repeat to yourself 'I have read the works of Marx, Engels, Lenin and Mao' that means nothing if you don't use your knowledge in practice. Knowledge without practice remains a pure philosophical theory, as in Kant and writers like that. For example, conversations you can have in the café in the evening, hotly debated theoretically and seriously thought out and really interesting, can evaporate the following morning and just leave a faint stale aftertaste, if they don't lead to a connection with working practice. I'm not just thinking about film work, but work with workers and peasants and situations where you see yourself confronted with the practice of life.

The people you work with have to be able to realise that you're a worker too – with your hands and with your head. This is something that young film-makers often don't have.

Lots of people come to see me and say to me, 'Joris Ivens, couldn't you give me some advice?' Young people come to see me from all over the world. It's very difficult to give advice to young film-makers when you don't know

119

what sort of life they lead, what they think, how they act politically – and what their working conditions are like. To be a film-maker is a very appealing job. If you have a modicum of talent, you can soon get yourself a position, an advanced reputation, and you can earn lots of money. And there is a real danger there of being corrupted. Obviously, there's corruption everywhere, but in their business it is particularly seductive. In our job you have got to be very strong in a way if you don't want to go under and become commercial. For everyone there is a moment in his life when he has to choose for sure, when he has to decide. Which way will you go? Which road will you take? I know this myself, and I have known such moments several times in my life. For example when I had an offer in 1934 to make a film about radio. It was a real propaganda film for Philips. During the shooting I had to fight furiously to get the freedom that had been promised me. I had been given a contract which stated quite clearly that I could do what I wanted and that I would not be subject to any external control. It was a contract guaranteeing full autonomy. A few people, very few, get an opportunity like that, those sorts of working conditions, and they go under immediately. One has absolutely to struggle fiercely against the attractiveness of it, because who are we doing it for? When you get a contract like that, and accept it, you're taking a risk . . . If you make the film and make a good job of it, you have an easy path in front of you. You make this film, you go on making films of the same type and so on . . . In the world of the film business that's very easy. This corrupt side of cinema pursues you everywhere. I don't know the concrete situation in West Germany today, but I know what it's like for film-makers in Holland, France and Italy and I've seen a lot of people go under [. . .]

For the younger generation of film-makers I think the choice to be made is harder than it was for us, in our day. Why? Perhaps it was easier for us because the dividing lines were clearer. We saw the enemy clearly. Over there were the capitalists, and over here were we, the communists, the revolutionaries.

Q: Do you think the reality of that image has changed?
A: Yes, in a sense. I think the enemy, today, is much more hidden, more subtle, and that people are less well-informed. There are no clear ideas. For example, lots of people still think that the 'socialism' of the Soviet Union really is the socialism we want – or that German social democracy might be it, or might not but might still be the lesser evil because after all it does still represent the workers' interest in spite of everything. Or take the French socialists, or even worse the French Communist Party which is straightfor-wardly abolishing the dictatorship of the proletariat. They've got nothing else in their minds except running after votes. But whose votes, I'd like to know? Perhaps I'm wrong. I'm not really a great one for theory [. . .]

My reply to lots of young film-makers has been, 'Look at the richness of life and the people who are dying of poverty. Show their struggle!' and they've said to me, 'No, we want to make fiction films.' 'All right then, make fiction films; you'll make lots of money. But the compromises you're going to have to make will be greater. You haven't only got the State against you, and ideological conservatism, but you've got big capital against you, the banks for example. On the other hand in documentary film you've got less money, but more freedom.' In spite of everything the fiction film has an enormous appeal and is sometimes considered the original artistic form of cinema.

Q: The representatives of the French New Wave and the young German cinema have completely different political conceptions. Some time back they each chose the path they wanted to take. For most of them it was the established path, committed but comfortable. But never the path of the revolutionary film-maker. And for that reason the decision is not documentary or fiction film, but socialist film or bourgeois film.

A: Don't get me wrong. The fiction film is a marvellous form of cinema. In documentaries, in the same way as in fiction films, you can lie or you can tell the truth. It's up to you. For someone who wants to work in an independent and revolutionary way, the path of fiction film-making is completely

Le peuple et ses fusils

121

blocked. In the documentary field there are more possibilities for revolutionary work. You can make fewer compromises and can allow yourself to tell the truth.

Q: That seems an odd judgment. What is it based on?
A: On the reasons I have already given. With a fiction film you have to make a lot of money, that is you've got to make it back for the people who give it to you, the banks and so on. All the money that goes into the production of a film is a burden on your back, you're bent double under the weight of it. Ask the film-makers of the young German cinema, they know this better than I do. All the crazy struggles that you have to get into . . . I'm not a fanatic of documentary film; I see all the art of cinema as one big pit – fiction film, documentary film, news film and mixtures of these three genres. It all depends on who you are addressing, what you are talking about, why you say precisely this and not that, and what style you adopt. My films have very different styles. But in spite of that, after 5 or 6 minutes you can tell that the film is one of mine. A film like *The People and their Guns* is a didactic film – which is obvious. But *How Yukong Moved the Mountains* is quite different. In this film about China Marceline Loridan and I withdraw completely. There is very little commentary, the images speak for themselves and the Chinese people speak with their own voice. The commentary adds very little in the way of depth. It's the dialogues which give depth, the discussions. Or take a film like *Pour le Mistral*. In my opinion it's a very lyrical film. It encapsulates and expresses a little bit of revolutionary nature. In this film everyone can think their own revolution, or recognise their love, or live their struggle against nature.

Q: One might say that films like the Yukong *series or* Borinage *are films that lean towards the documentary pole, but given their political testimony and the revolutionary 'red thread' that runs through them, they are also films which perform a* mise en scène.
A: My films can't be categorised that easily and put into little boxes. But they can all be called documentaries.

Bibliography

Grelier's *Joris Ivens* and the booklet produced by the Amsterdam Film-museum *Joris Ivens, 50 Jaar Wereldcineast* both contain extensive bibliographies about Ivens. The purpose of the bibliography which follows is to give an indication of works consulted in the process of compiling this publication, and to provide a starting point for others interested in investigating Ivens' work. Most, but not all, of the works referred to are available in the British Film Institute Library. The main restriction is linguistic. The list is notably restricted to French, Italian and English text, with a few exceptions. This is a result of my own linguistic limits. Yet even within those limits, it is remarkable that so little has been written about Joris Ivens in English, and this emerges clearly from the bibliography. It appears symptomatic of a certain gap in relation to aspects of the documentary tradition, but also a testament to the power of censorship.

A. Published film scripts etc., by Ivens and collaborators
Joris IVENS, *Zuiderzee*, (ed.) Corrado Terzi, Poligono Società, Milan 1945.
Joris IVENS and Vladimir POZNER, *Lied der Ströme*, Tribüne, Berlin 1957.
Jacques PREVERT, *La Seine a rencontré Paris, Cinéma 60* n46, May 1960, pp45-49.
Joris IVENS, '*A Valparaiso:* Court métrage de Joris Ivens', *L'Avant-Scène du Cinéma* n76, December 1967, pp50-57.
    '*A Valparaiso:* fiche filmographique', (ed.) G. Gauthier, *Image et Son* n183, April 1965.
Joris IVENS, [Rotterdam Europoort] '*Europort: Rotterdam:* Court métrage de Joris Ivens', *L'Avant-Scène du Cinéma* n99, January 1970, pp43-48.
J-C. ULRICH, *Le ciel, la terre* (commentary), *Positif* n76, June 1966.
Marceline LORIDAN and Joris IVENS, *Le 17è parallèle, la guerre du peuple (deux mois sous la terre)*. Editeurs Français Réunis, Paris 1968.
Joris IVENS, [Le peuple et ses fusils] *Il popolo e i suoi fucili*, Samonà e Savelli, Rome 1970.

B. Writings by Ivens and collaborators
Joris IVENS, *The Camera and I*, Seven Seas, Berlin 1969.
    'Apprentice to Films, 1', *Theatre Arts*, March 1946, pp179-86.
    'Apprentice to Films, 2', *Theatre Arts*, April 1946, pp244-51.
    '*Borinage* – a Documentary Experience', *Film Culture*, v2 n1, 1956, pp6-11.
    'Collaboration in Documentary', *Films* (New York) 1/2, Spring 1940, pp30-42.
    'The Documentary Film and Morale', *Writers' Congress*, University of California, Berkeley 1944, pp75-79.
    'Une Déclaration de Joris Ivens à propos de "l'affaire des dix" ', *L'Ecran Français* n253, May 1950, p3.

'Making Documentary Films in China', *China Reconstructs*, January 1959, pp17-19.

'Notes', *Artsept* n2, April-June 1963.

'Notes on Hollywood', *New Theatre* III, 28 October 1936.

'Quelques réflexions sur les documentaires d'avant-garde', *La Revue des Vivants*, October 1931, pp518-20.

'Subjektivität und Montage', *Deutsche Filmkunst*, 1962, pp424-26.

'Vive le Cinéma Vérité', *Les Lettres Françaises*, March 1963.

Helen VAN DONGEN, 'Notes on the Making of *Louisiana Story*', extensively quoted in 'Imaginative Documentary', in K. Reisz and G. Millar, *The Technique of Film Editing* (cit.infra).

Other texts by Ivens and his collaborators are to be found in various anthologies and other works, cited in Section F of this bibliography.

C. Interviews with Ivens and collaborators

Ben ACHTENBERG, 'Helen van Dongen: an interview', *Film Quarterly*, Winter 1976/77, pp46-57.

R. BELLOUR and J. MICHAUD, '*Cuba Sí*: à propos de *Carnet de voyage* et *Peuple armé* de Joris Ivens', *Cinéma 61* n56, May 1961, pp45-50.

[BIANCO E NERO] Interview with Morando Morandini, *Bianco e nero*, 1964.

G. BRETT, 'We give you what we saw', interview with Joris Ivens and Marceline Loridan, in *China Now*, n70, March 1977, pp3-6.

S. DANEY, T. GIRAUD and S. PÉRON, '*Comment Yukong déplaça les montagnes:* entretien avec Joris Ivens et Marceline Loridan', *Cahiers du Cinéma* ns 266/67, May 1976, pp5–23.

J-M. DOUBLET and J-P. SERGENT, 'China on film – unrehearsed; film-makers Joris Ivens and Marceline Loridan work from the script of everyday life', *New China* v4 n2, Summer 1978, pp13-18.

Guy GAUTHIER, 'Un cinéma sous les bombes', interview with Joris Ivens back from Vietnam, *Image et Son* n187, October 1965, pp41-43.

'Le 17è parallèle', *Image et Son* n218, June-July 1968, pp111-120.

'Entretien avec Joris Ivens, Marceline Loridan et Jean-Pierre Sergent', *Image et Son* n237, March 1970, pp106-112.

Robert GRELIER, Interview with Joris Ivens, *Positif* n76, June 1966, pp42-53.

Guy HENNEBELLE, Interview with Joris Ivens, Marceline Loridan and Jean-Pierre Sergent, *Cinéma 70* n143, February 1970, pp80-89.

[IMAGE ET SON] 'Entretien avec Joris Ivens', *Image et Son* n173, Numéro Spécial 16mm, May 1964.

[IVENS and STORCK] '*Borinage* de Joris Ivens et Henri Storck: à propos d'un film social', *Documents* n9, January 1934, pp18-24.

Alexandra KLUGE and Bion STEINBORN, Interviews with Joris Ivens and Marceline Loridan, in *Filmfaust* I, 1/2, December 1976, pp6-51; and I, 4, June-July 1977, pp17-32.

Marcel MARTIN, 'Entretien avec Joris Ivens', *Cinéma 69* n133, February 1969, pp48-63.

Luce SAND, Interview with Joris Ivens, *Jeune Cinéma* n30, April 1968, pp10-12.

D. Books on Ivens and his work

[CENTRE POMPIDOU] *Joris Ivens: cinquante ans de cinéma*, (ed.) J–L. Passek, Centre National d'Art et de Culture Georges Pompidou, Paris 1979.

Cinéma Politique, Special Number 'Joris Ivens', Paris November 1978.

Claire DEVARRIEUX, *Entretien avec Joris Ivens*, Collection Ça Cinéma, Editions Albatros, Paris 1979 (the full text of a series of interviews with Ivens first published in *Le Monde* at the end of 1978).

[FILMMUSEUM AMSTERDAM] *Joris Ivens, 50 Jaar Wereldcineast*, Nederlands Filmmuseum Amsterdam 1978 (contains extensive and up-to-date bibliography).

Robert GRELIER, *Joris Ivens*, Editeurs Français Réunis, Paris 1965 (contains extensive bibliography).

W. KLAUE, M. LICHTENSTEIN and H. WEGNER, *Joris Ivens*, Staatliches Filmarchiv der DDR, Berlin 1963.

Klaus KREIMEIER, *Joris Ivens: ein Filmer an den Fronten der Weltrevolution*, Oberbaumverlag, Berlin 1976 (also in Italian as *Il cinema di Joris Ivens*, Mazzotta, Milan 1977).

A. ZALZMAN, *Joris Ivens*, Seghers, Paris 1963. Introduction by Georges Sadoul.

E. Articles and pamphlets

R. BENAYOUN, A. BOLDUC, M. CIMENT and others, 'Débat', *Positif* n113, February 1970, pp11-27.

G-P. BERNAGOZZI, 'Ivens: dall' "avanguardia" al "realismo" come forma di pensiero', in A. Ferrero, *Storia del Cinema*, Marsilio, Venice 1978, vol III, pp39-52.

J. DEMEURE, 'L'automobile de Joris Ivens', *Positif* n76, June 1966, pp63-67.

Cathérine DUNCAN, 'The First Years', *Sight and Sound*, Spring 1950, pp37-39.

G. FERRARA, article on Ivens, followed by debate, *Filmcritica* ns39-40.

Guy GAUTHIER, '*Comment Yukong déplaça les montagnes*', *Image et Son* n305, April 1976, pp78-83.

G. GOZLAN, Review of Grelier and Zalzman books on Ivens, *Positif* n74, April 1966, pp143ff.

Cynthia GRENIER, 'Joris Ivens: social realist versus lyric poet', *Sight and Sound*, Autumn 1958, pp204-207.

Richard GRIFFITH, 'Helen van Dongen', *New Movies* (National Board of Review Magazine), New York, November-December 1943, pp26-28.

J. S. HAMILTON, 'Joris Ivens', *New Movies*, May 1936.

Bert HOGENKAMP, *Workers' Newsreels in the 1920s and 1930s*, History Group of the Communist Party, London 1977 (contains discussion of VVVC Journal, 1930-31).

Joris Ivens e i problemi del film documentario, Modena 1978 (publication in Italian in pamphlet form of an essay from *Joris Ivens: 50 Jaar Wereldcineast*, Amsterdam 1978).

'Ivens, Storck en de Club de l'Ecran', *Skrien* n66, July-August 1977, pp21-22.

J-P. LAJOURNADE et al, '*Comment Yukong déplaça les montagnes*', *Cinéthique* ns23/24, 1977, pp100-111.

Henri LANGLOIS, 'Joris Ivens', *L'Avant-Scène du Cinéma* n182, February 1977, pp38-39.

Jean LENAUER, 'Report from Belgium and Holland', *Close Up*, June 1928, pp26-30.

'The Cinema in Paris', *Close Up*, January 1929, pp66-70.

Herbert MARSHALL, 'Moscow overtakes and surpasses', *Experimental Cinema* n5, 1934, pp41-42.

Lino MICCICHÉ, 'Un poeta della "macchina da presa" ', *Cinema Documentario*, April-June 1966.
Pierre MICHAUT, 'Joris Ivens', article in three parts, *Cahiers du Cinéma*, n25, July 1953, pp5-11; n26, August-September 1953, pp26-30; n28, November 1953, pp20-30.
Léon MOUSSINAC, 'Joris Ivens: discours', *Artsept* n2, April-June 1963, pp22-23.
S. PÉRON, 'Ivens et Chine', *Cahiers du Cinéma* ns266/67, May 1976, pp24-29.
P-L. THIRARD, 'Un cinéma différent; *La Jetée – A Valparaiso*', *Positif* ns64/65, [Autumn] 1964, pp144-45.
Tom WAUGH, '*How Yukong moved the mountains*: filming the cultural revolution', *Jump Cut* ns12/13, December 1976, pp3-6.
E. YEVTUCHENKO, 'Joris Ivens' (poem), *Positif* n76, June 1966.

F. Other works
Bela BALAZS, *Theory of the Film*, Dennis Dobson, London 1952.
Richard BARSAM, *Non-Fiction Film: a critical history*, Dutton, New York 1973 (contains J. Ivens, 'Spain and *The Spanish Earth*' (1969), pp349-75).
Hanns EISLER, *Composing for the Films*, Dennis Dobson, London 1947.
Forsyth HARDY (ed.) *Grierson on Documentary*, Faber and Faber, London 1966.
L. FURHAMMAR and F. ISAKSSON, *Politics and Film*, Studio Vista, London 1971.
Lewis JACOBS, *The Documentary Tradition*, Hopkinson and Blake, New York 1971 (contains S. Meyers and J. Leyda, 'Joris Ivens, artist in documentary'; M. Losey 'Joris Ivens' *Power and the Land*'; and Joris Ivens, 'The Making of *Rain*').
Jay LEYDA, *Voices of Film Experience*, Macmillan, New York 1977 (contains contribution by Ivens).
Kino, Allen and Unwin, London, 1960.
G. MARSOLAIS, 'L'aventure du cinéma direct', Seghers, Paris 1964 (contains interview with Joris Ivens and Henri Storck).
V. POZNER, *Vladimir Pozner se souvient*, Juilliard, Paris 1972.
Karel REISZ and Gavin MILLAR, *The Technique of Film Editing*, Focal Press, London 1968.
Georges SADOUL, *Dictionary of Film-makers*, University of California, Berkeley 1972.
Dictionary of Films, University of California, Berkeley 1972.
William STOTT, *Documentary Expression and Thirties America*, OUP, New York 1976.
Dziga VERTOV, *Articles, journaux, projets*, translation and notes by Sylviane Mossé and Andrée Robel, Collection 10:18, Cahiers du Cinéma, Paris 1972.

Joris Ivens – Film Availability in Britain

The following Ivens films are currently available for rental within the United Kingdom. Certain versions are incomplete, as indicated. In conjunction with the publication of this book and the National Film Theatre retrospective, BFI Film Availability Services plans to bring into distribution further titles. Details of new acquisitions and restored versions will be published in due course. Advice on availability may be obtained from the Central Booking Agency, a section of Film Availability Services, 127 Charing Cross Road, London WC2H 0EA.

Title	Gauge	Distributor	Address
Rain	35/16	BFI	127 Charing Cross Rd London WC2H OEA
Misère au Borinage	16 (sound version)	Workers Film Association	38 Dartmouth Park Rd London NW5
New Earth	16/35 (last reel censored)	BFI	
Indonesia Calling		Contemporary Films	55 Greek Street London W1
Song of the Rivers	35	Educational & Television Films	247a Upper Street London N1
Before Spring	35	ETV	
. . . A Valparaiso	16	Essential	Concord Films Council 201 Felixstowe Road Ipswich, Suffolk
Threatening Sky	16	Contemporary. Films	
Loin du Vietnam	16/35	Contemporary Films	
17th Parallel	16 (last reels missing)	The Other Cinema	12/13 Little Newport St London WC2
How Yukong Moved the Mountains	16	The Other Cinema	

Printed in Britain by Tonbridge Printers Limited, Tonbridge, Kent.